Free to Read
A Guide to Effective Reading
Revised Edition

Henry A. Bamman
Professor of Education
California State University
Sacramento

Midori F. Hiyama
Reading Specialist
Instructor of English
Sacramento City College

Delbert L. Prescott
Reading Specialist
Instructor of English
Sacramento City College

**The Benjamin/Cummings
Publishing Company**
Menlo Park, California
Reading, Massachusetts
London • Amsterdam
Don Mills, Ontario • Sydney

Acknowledgments

For permission to reprint material in this textbook, grateful acknowledgment is made to the following sources:

"Say It, but Mean It" by David Newman and Robert Benton, from "Man Talk," *Mademoiselle* Magazine, December 1967.

"Where Will the Jobs Be?" adapted from "Where Will the Jobs Be?" In *Nation's Business*, March 1972. Courtesy of *Nations Business*.

Greyhound timetable by courtesy of Greyhound Lines.

Map of Sacramento, basic map reproduced by permission of the California State Automobile Association, copyright owner.

"Beating those Blue-Collar Blues" by Trevor Ambrister. Reprinted with permission from the April 1973 *Reader's Digest*. Copyright 1973 by The Reader's Digest Assn., Inc.

"Big Job of Job Hunting," reprinted by permission from *Senior Scholastic*, © 1964 by Scholastic Magazines, Inc.

"Miracle Drugs" from *Miracle Drugs and the New Age of Medicine* by Fred Reinfeld, © 1962 by Sterling Publishing Co., Inc., New York 10016.

"Vitamin Overdose" adapted from "Vitamin Oversell" by Wendy Burrell. All reasonable attempts have been made to contact the author, but this has regrettably proved impossible.

"A Directory of Drugs" from *Drugs*. By permission of the California Delinquency Prevention Commission.

"Urban Noise" adapted from "Noise, A Syndrome of Modern Society," by Clifford R. Bragdon, in *Scientist and Citizen*, March 1968. © *Environment* 1968.

"Laser Beams" adapted from "Lasers, the Light Fantastic," by Max Gunther, in *Playboy*, February 1968; by permission of the author and HMH Publishing Co.

"Oh, Smart Man" adapted from "My Southwest" by Esther Henderson from *Arizona Highways*, January 1968.

"A Vision of the Year 2000" adapted from "A Vision of the Year 2000" by Clare Boothe Luce from *McCalls*, January 1966. By permission of Clare Boothe Luce.

"Right or Wrong?" and "Why Fear?" reprinted from "Say No to Your Kids—They'll Love You For It" by Ann Landers in the June, 1968, issue of *Family Circle*. © The Family Circle, Inc. 1968. By permission of Ann Landers, Publishers-Hall Syndicate.

Table of contents from Doris Wilcox Gilbert, *Breaking the Reading Barrier*, © 1959, Prentice-Hall, Inc. By permission.

"The Thin Grey Line" adapted from "The Thin Grey Line" by Marya Mannes, in *McCalls*, January 1964. Reprinted by permission of Harold Ober Associates Incorporated. Copyright © 1963 by Marya Mannes.

"More Air Than Corn" from "Movie House Popcorn is Mostly Air," The Sacramento *Bee*, November 13, 1968.

Webster's entry under "folk" from *Webster's New World Dictionary of the American Language*, College Edition. Copyright 1968 by The World Publishing Company, Cleveland, Ohio.

Racing score chart reprinted from *Sports Car Graphic* Magazine—Peterson Publishing Co.

"Changing Beliefs about Women" adapted from Our Bodies Ourselves, copyright 1971, 1973 by the Boston Women's Health Book Collective, Inc. Reprinted by permission of Simon and Schuster.

"Appeal to Justice" from Peithmann, Irvin M., *Broken Peace Pipes*, 1964. Courtesy of Charles C. Thomas, Publisher, Springfield, Illinois.

"The Myth of Race" adapted by permission of The World Publishing Company from *Man's Most Dangerous Myth* by Ashley Montagu. Copyright © 1964 by Ashley Montagu.

"Some Uncomfortable Questions" adapted from "Some Uncomfortable Questions," by Loudon Wainwright, *Life* Magazine, April 26, 1968, © 1968 Time Inc.

"A Testament of Hope" adapted from an article that originally appeared in *Playboy* magazine; copyright © 1968 by the Estate of Martin Luther King, Jr. By permission of Joan Daves.

"The Magic Kingdom" adapted from "The Magic Kingdom," *Time*, April 15, 1966. Courtesy *Time* The Weekly Newsmagazine; Copyright Time Inc. 1966.

© 1975 by Cummings Publishing Company, Inc. Philippines Copyright 1975.

Printed in the United States of America. Published simultaneously in Canada. Library of Congress Catalog Card Number 74-84819.

ISBN 0-8465-5835-1
FGHIJKL-AL-79

**Cummings Publishing Company, Inc.
2727 Sand Hill Rd., Menlo Park,
California 94025**

Preface

Good reading is far more than recognizing words in print, far more than merely recalling main ideas and related details. Good reading calls for active participation of the reader in reacting to the ideas set forth by the writer and in extending beyond the page to establish relationships with previous knowledge and experience. Certainly being a good reader is basic to becoming well educated.

Free to Read is a text in developmental reading for youth and adults who are concerned about improving their basic reading skills. High school and community college students who are looking forward to vocations or to academic careers will find that the carefully planned sequence of lessons will provide them with a means of testing their reading proficiency and developing skills that can be transferred to all types of reading. The topics are timely and interesting to youth and young adults alike: people, values, jobs, personal decisions, controversial issues, and man's dreams and achievements.

The exercises in this text have been developed to meet the needs of individuals or of groups of students. Carefully sequenced exercises provide entry points for the individual who has determined a personal need for improvement.

Henry A. Bamman
Midori F. Hiyama
Delbert L. Prescott

Contents

Unit Seven: They Work to Win

Unit Eight: Men Apart

Unit Nine: Well Known

Appendix

I, a Person

I think I could turn and live awhile with the animals...
    they are so placid and self-contained,
I stand and look at them sometimes half the day long.
They do not sweat and whine about their condition,
They do not lie awake in the dark and weep
    for their sins,
They do not make me sick discussing their duty to God,
Not one is dissatisfied...not one is demented with the
    mania of owning things
Not one kneels to another nor to his kind that lived
    thousands of years ago,
Not one is respectable or industrious over the
    whole earth.
                    WALT WHITMAN, "Song of Myself"

How to Read a Paragraph

Skim through the pages of this book and you will see that it contains short articles and long articles about many subjects. Some of the articles are crammed with information; other articles simply provide entertainment. But whether you read for enjoyment or to obtain information, you will get more out of your reading if you understand a few facts about paragraphs.

A paragraph is a part of a large composition. There are no rules that say how long a paragraph must be. It may consist of a single sentence or several sentences. The important thing to remember is that a paragraph develops one idea of a larger topic. It's up to you, the reader, to discover what that main idea is.

Usually the main idea of a paragraph is found in a single sentence, which is called the topic sentence. A topic sentence may be the first or second sentence of a paragraph, or it may be the last sentence. These two positions are the most common. There are, however, other places where a topic sentence may be found. Sometimes the topic sentence appears in the middle of the paragraph. Or the topic sentence may be split, half of it appearing at the beginning of the paragraph and the other half at the end.

All the other sentences in a paragraph relate in some way to the topic sentence. They may repeat the topic sentence for added emphasis; present statements that show what the topic is not; define through detail, example, or illustration; or point out a result or consequence.

In well-written paragraphs the author states the main idea and tells what points will be developed. Not all paragraphs, however, will have clearly identifiable main ideas. It is up to you to discover the connection between the main idea and the other sentences. Looking closely at a few well-written paragraphs should make you more aware of the author's syle and purpose. (323 words)

Sound Sense: Vowels

Has it ever occurred to you that if you could recognize in print all the words you knew how to use in speech, your reading problems would be all but solved?

Beginning with this exercise and others like it, you will find valuable hints on how to pronounce difficult words. You should study them very carefully, because understanding them will lead to increasing your reading skills. The rules you will find are NOT to be memorized; they are first to be understood, and referred to as many times as necessary, until they become second nature to you.

Sometimes, these exercises will seem of no importance—a waste of time. THEY ARE NOT. If you're uncertain about their value, you would be cheating yourself if you didn't take the matter up with an expert: your instructor. Doing these exercises carefully under his close supervision will bring favorable results not only in your reading, but also in your writing and spelling.

Say each of the words below. Notice that the vowels in the first row stand for short sounds, and in the second row, for long sounds.

get	pick	on	and	think	ask	us	wish
he	go	by	we	flu	she	fro	hi

Circle the correct answer for each statement.

1. If the only vowel in a word is at the beginning or in the middle, the vowel is usually (short, long).
2. If the only vowel in a word is at the end, the vowel is usually (short, long).

In the words below, put this mark ⁻ over each long vowel; put this mark ˇ over each short vowel. For example: hăt, mē.

3. not   6. is   9. stand   12. when   15. shock   18. thatch

4. fun   7. he   10. cinch   13. spry   16. tempt   19. wrench

5. wry   8. at   11. brink   14. clog   17. sty   20. stunt

Key Words
reaction–action in response to an influence; *mold*–to shape or form;
revenge–returning evil for evil

Reaction to Criticism

Since criticism may be positive as well as negative, people who criticize us often think they are helping us. Parents sometimes feel it is their duty to correct the errors of their children. They think this is what makes them "parents." Some teachers think of criticism as an important part of their job. They look at students as raw material to mold into educated adults. Criticism seems to be a right of employers as a means of improving their employees. And, of course, brothers and sisters and even friends frequently feel they have been given the right to correct faults in others.

There are many ways of reacting to personal criticism by others. First, we may choose to deny it. We simply say that it is untrue and refuse to listen. Second, we often try to defend ourselves with detailed explanations of the behavior being criticized. A third reaction is to attack the person who has criticized us. We usually begin by criticizing him. Still another way is to react by accepting the criticism and saying that we are worse than what was said. Yet another typical reaction is to withdraw in anger, and we may even secretly plot revenge against the person who criticized us. (203 words)

Check It

Go back and read; then underline the topic sentence in each paragraph.

Sound Sense: Vowels

1. Say these words below. How many vowels are in each word? _____

2. How many vowels are pronounced in each word? _____

brain	soak	beat	suit	steam	paid
break	pain	roam	weak	fruit	steak

3. Now underline the correct words that complete this statement: When two vowels come together in a word, one vowel usually stands for the (short, long, silent) sound and one of the vowels is (long, silent, short).

Remember: The most common exceptions to the above rule are *au, aw, ew, ow, ou, oi, oy,* and *ea.*

Mark the vowels in the words below. Put this mark ˘ over vowels that have a short sound; put this mark ˉ over vowels that have a long sound; and put this mark / through vowels that are silent. For example: dāte̸, fa̸st.

4. plant	16. sold	28. silo	40. grain
5. rely	17. she	29. seal	41. ecstatic
6. lunch	18. fry	30. faint	42. real
7. lamb	19. post	31. repeat	43. tails
8. solo	20. silk	32. sty	44. instruct
9. rodent	21. alto	33. maintain	45. lean
10. dry	22. brush	34. exclaim	46. loaf
11. flat	23. brain	35. clean	47. weak
12. ring	24. lash	36. comb	48. road
13. shrink	25. flesh	37. peach	49. coach
14. cupid	26. pry	38. misgivings	50. pain
15. duck	27. tell	39. explain	

Key Words

entail-to require; *recipient*-a person who receives something; *facet*-a distinct part; *incalculable*-too great in number to be counted; *symbolically*-standing for an idea

---

Say It, but Mean It

David Newman and Robert Benton

Directions: *Read as rapidly as possible to determine the main idea.*

To really love somebody, with all that entails, is a piece of work. Those few people you love are the recipients of your responsibility. You will break your back for them, put up with them at their worst, stop doing what you want to do if they need your comfort or strength or company. The facets of love are incalculable. You don't say "I love you" lightly—not if you have a brain in your head, you don't. Because once you make that commitment, you are altering your life and the life of the one you love.

This is real love we're talking about, the kind that gets tested 24 hours a day, seven days a week, not the kind that gives a flower to a stranger on the street. All the rewards in that action are for the giver, not the receiver. You got the flower? Swell. Sniff it, hold it for a while, throw it away. But the cat that gives it to you is terribly content with himself, quite sure that he has symbolically performed a love act. He can eat off that for days. But what he really did was to give you a flower. He wears LOVE on his forehead, but he makes no sacrifice, feels no pain, gives up no freedom, takes on no responsibility. (221 words)

Check It

Check the sentence that best expresses the main idea.

___ 1. Giving flowers to another is one form of love.

___ 2. The facets of love are easy to determine.

___ 3. To really love someone, you must be willing to give as well as to receive.

___ 4. Giving a flower to another is a real sacrifice.

___ 5. In real love you may say "I love you" lightly and still mean it.

Sound Sense: Vowels

Say each of the pairs of words below.

bit	rat	rod	cut	kit
bite	rate	rode	cute	kite

What does the final *e* do to the vowel before it in each word? Did you notice that the final *e* is silent?

Circle each word below that has a long vowel.

race	bat	fine	tone	made	tube
these	game	this	rub	time	those

Context Clues

You can often figure out the meaning of an unfamiliar word when you see it alongside familiar words in a sentence. This is called *using context clues,* or, in other words, making an educated guess. This may not work all the time, but if you learn a few important clues you can attack many unknown words and learn their meanings. Here are four different context clues to look for when you become stuck on an unknown word.

Definition. Often the writer will actually tell you what the word means by definition. He may reveal a word's meaning by providing an explanatory synonym, phrase, clause, or entire sentence. He may define by example, using such expressions as *for example, for instance,* and *such as,* or such punctuation marks as parentheses, semicolons, commas, and dashes. For example:

The old train depot is now *defunct;* there is no trace of it, even though the tracks still run through town.

The prisoner was *harassed*—annoyed continually—by his jailers.

Contrast. A contrast clue in a sentence tells what a word does *not* mean. This can be done with a single word (an antonym), a group of words, or an entire sentence. Often such words as *however*, *yet*, and *not* signal contrast clues. For example:

> The morning audience greeted the speaker very coldly, giving him very little praise; however, following his afternoon presentation, he received *commendations* from the group.

> The newcomer liked the friendliness of his old neighborhood, not the *harassment* of his neighbors in his new surroundings.

Experience. Past experience may allow you to guess the meaning of the unknown word. If you are already familiar with a situation described in a sentence, the unfamiliar word may become clear to you. For example:

> Old Joe was afraid to walk into the *decrepit* house since the floor sagged and creaked with every step.

> Any young mother of five small children feels very *harassed* by the end of the day.

Summary. A summary-type clue sums up a familiar situation or idea with a word or phrase usually found at the end of the sentence. For example:

> Julie can participate in any activity. She excels in swimming and golfing; she prepares gourmet dishes in no time at all; she sews all her clothes—in fact, she's a *versatile* teen-ager.

> When reporters continually questioned the President on minor points of his foreign policy statement, he felt *harassed*.

9

Words You Need

Test your skill in using context clues. Read each sentence and choose the meaning of the word in italics. Write the letter of your answer on the line. Use your dictionary if necessary.

___ 1. Of all the brilliant colors in the landscape, green was the most *predominant*; the grass, the trees, and the bushes were all shades of green.
Predominant means a) most noticeable; b) most beautiful; c) least noticeable.

___ 2. The governor appeared on television and *proclaimed* our flooded city a disaster area.
Proclaimed means a) predicted; b) proved; c) announced officially.

___ 3. Many of the early settlers in the New England colonies had English *ancestors*.
Ancestors means a) antiques; b) people from whom one is descended; c) customs.

___ 4. The young scout was awarded many *decorations* for his good deeds.
Decorations means a) ornaments; b) trimmings; c) medals of honor.

___ 5. When the United States *annexed* Texas in 1845, a great deal of land was added to this country.
Annexed means a) added one thing to a larger thing; b) sold; c) discovered.

___ 6. Because our college has students from many foreign countries, we have a *polyglot* student body.
Polyglot means a) steady; b) changing; c) speaking several languages.

___ 7. Our city is very safe; we have a *minimum* number of crimes every year.
Minimum means a) greatest amount possible; b) least amount possible; c) average amount.

___ 8. After Marie won the tennis match, she was *besieged* by fans asking for her autograph.
Besieged means a) congratulated; b) overwhelmed with requests; c) beaten.

___ 9. The swim team gained *prominence* all over the state by winning many of the swim meets this summer.
Prominence means a) state of being widely and favorably known; b) first place; c) promotions.

___10. Ron is such a *bigot;* he just won't listen to anyone who disagrees with him.
Bigot means a) talkative person; b) pest; c) narrow-minded person.

___11. The *contemptuous* stares of the richly dressed people made me feel very uncomfortable in my blue jeans and sneakers.
Contemptuous means a) looking down on, scornful; b) envious; c) admiring.

___12. My *colleagues* at the office helped me finish the work on time.
Colleagues means a) college students; b) fellow workers; c) customers.

Hawaii to Washington: Daniel K. Inouye

"Dan Inouye has lived by the code of personal courage on the battlefield, and in the political arena. He has faced the aggressor's bullets, and the bigot's contemptuous stare. He has gained the admiration and respect of his fellowmen. Even more important, he has, by his example and witness, helped to make the hearts of his fellowmen more tolerant, more free of the awful burden of racism. I believe that this story will become part of the heritage of our nation, inspiring others to find within themselves the strength to say 'There isn't a thing in the world I couldn't do—if I want to badly enough.' "

These words were written by President Lyndon B. Johnson. They are taken from the foreword to *Journey to Washington,* the autobiography of Daniel Ken Inouye (ē nō ´wā).

Daniel Inouye was born of Japanese parents in Honolulu in 1924. The eldest of four children, Dan's life was no different from any other Nisei* boy living in the predominantly Japanese neighborhoods in Honolulu. But on December 7, 1941, that fateful day when Japanese bombs fell on Pearl Harbor, Dan's life changed.

Dedicated Japanese-Americans had a burning desire to fight for the United States. But for two years they were not allowed to defend the land they loved. In fact, all Japanese living in America were suspected of possible disloyalty. Finally, in January 1943, they were given their chance. President Roosevelt proclaimed, "No loyal citizen of the United States should be denied the democratic right to exercise the responsibilities of his citizenship, regardless of his ancestry."

*Nisei (nē´sā): A native-born U.S. or Canadian citizen born of immigrant Japanese parents.

From the book *Journey to Washington,* by Senator Daniel K. Inouye with Lawrence Elliott. Copyright © 1967 by Prentice-Hall, Inc. Published by Prentice-Hall, Inc., Englewood Cliffs, New Jersey.

At once some 10,000 Nisei young men volunteered for the service. Dan was among the first to do so. He served in the legendary 442nd Regimental Combat Team, an outfit made up entirely of Nisei volunteers. With "Go For Broke!" as their battle cry, these soldiers fought bravely in Italy and France. The 442nd became one of the most decorated Army units in history.

The outfit came to be known by its motto, "Go For Broke!" The pidgin English phrase means to risk everything. To the men it meant to run an obstacle course as though their lives depended on it. It meant to march quick time until they were ready to drop, and then to break into a trot. It meant to give everything they had.

In battle Dan single-handedly knocked out two machine-gun nests while leading attacks. During action he was shot in the stomach, and his right arm was shattered by a grenade. For his heroism Dan received the Congressional Medal of Honor, the Distinguished Service Cross, and fourteen other decorations. When he was discharged in 1947, he was a captain. Now when asked if he would defend America, Dan holds up his empty sleeve and answers, "The country can have the other one, too."

Daniel Inouye's courage never failed him. After leaving the Army, he returned home to study. Before the war Dan had intended to study medicine, but the loss of his right arm caused him to go into law. At the University of Hawaii he majored in government and economics. Later he attended George Washington University Law School in Washington, D.C. He was a member of the board of editors of the *George Washington Law Review* and received his degree in 1952. While he was a student, Dan married Margaret Awamura, a speech teacher. After finishing law school, Dan returned home. He worked in the government of the Territory of Hawaii until the islands became a state.

The Hawaiian Islands were annexed by the United States in 1898. They were organized as a territory in 1900. For years the people of the islands tried to get statehood for Hawaii. But some Congressmen were against statehood because of Hawaii's racial composition. Due to Hawaii's location in the

Pacific Ocean, the islands have a polyglot population. However, the Hawaiian Islands also have a reputation for practicing a minimum of racial discrimination. And so the United States Congress finally passed a bill granting statehood to Hawaii. On August 21, 1959, Hawaii officially became the fiftieth state in the Union. Eight days later, Daniel Ken Inouye, World War II hero, lawyer, and former member of the territorial government of Hawaii, was sworn in as Hawaii's first U.S. Representative. By his election to the House of Representatives, Daniel Inouye became the first U.S. Congressman of Japanese ancestry.

When Dan Inouye was elected to Congress, he said, "Hawaii is much more interested in what we can contribute to the general welfare of the nation than what we expect the nation to contribute to us. I will do my best to see that Hawaii receives fair treatment as a state."

After being sworn into office, Dan had a talk with Sam Rayburn, the Speaker of the House:

"How does it feel to be a U.S. Congressman?" Mr. Rayburn asked.

"I'm very proud and very happy and a little scared, Mr. Speaker," Dan answered.

Speaker Rayburn nodded. "That's the way I felt. That's the way we all feel the first time, I guess. But there's no reason to be scared. If you're the right man, you'll do well, and if you're the wrong man . . . well, being scared won't keep you from being found out."

Dan served as a Congressman for three years. Then, on November 6, 1962, he was elected to the Senate.

When Dan had been sworn into the House of Representatives, his father had been unable to attend because of a heart attack. But when Dan was elected to the Senate, his father and his two brothers went to Washington to watch the ceremony. Afterward Dan received a telephone call from the White House. It was President John F. Kennedy congratulating Dan and asking him to bring his father and family to the White House the next day.

The following morning Dan, with his wife, father, and brothers, went into the Oval Room of the White House. There they spent a memorable half-hour with the President. When they left, they found a crowd of reporters waiting to ask questions of the new Senator. Dan said, "Gentlemen, this is not my day. The President invited my father to the White House, and I just happened to tag along. This is my father's day."

The reporters besieged Mr. Inouye with questions. When the rapid-fire questions stopped, Mr. Inouye spoke to them quietly but with great dignity.

"I want to thank the people of Hawaii for their goodness to my son," he said, "for sending him to the Senate. For me, for myself, I have seen my son become a Senator, I have been invited to eat with the Majority Leader of the Senate, and now I have met the President of the United States. Nothing that happens to me now can be greater. I will die a happy man."

In 1964, Inouye became the father of a much longed-for son, Daniel Ken, Jr. It was then that Senator Inouye agreed to write his autobiography so that he could set down for his son the record of his life up to that time. *Journey to Washington*, the autobiography written with Lawrence Elliott, begins with Dan's grandparents' decision to leave Japan to find a new life in Hawaii. It follows Dan's career to his position as United States Senator.

About his election to the Senate, Dan wrote these words:

"I was going to the Senate, to the highest reaches of my government; I, Dan Inouye, who had been raised in respectable poverty and whose father had been born in a tiny Japanese village. My face and eyes and shape would be different from those of my colleagues. I was not of the Western world. But the fact is that there was really not so great a difference between my story and the stories of millions of other Americans who had come to this land from Ireland and Italy and Poland and Greece. They had come because America would permit any man to aspire to the topmost limits of his own talent and energy. I am proud to be one with these people."(1349 words)

Time:_____

Check It: Fill in the blanks with the letter of the correct answer.

___ 1. The main idea of this selection is
  a) A war hero can become a United States Senator.
  b) Regardless of background, a person can achieve his or her goal through sheer determination and hard work.
  c) In politics it's a quick climb from lawyer to Congressman.

___ 2. Senator Daniel Inouye's parents were
  a) Japanese.
  b) Chinese.
  c) Hawaiian.

___ 3. The term *Nisei* refers to
  a) any U.S. citizen born of Japanese parents.
  b) any U.S. citizen born of immigrant Japanese parents.
  c) all Japanese born in Hawaii.

___ 4. "Go For Broke!" was the nickname of the Army unit composed of
  a) all Hawaiian-born volunteers.
  b) Nisei volunteers and draftees.
  c) all Nisei volunteers.

___ 5. Japanese-American young men were able to volunteer for the Army
  a) immediately after Pearl Harbor.
  b) only to serve at home.
  c) after President Roosevelt's proclamation of January 1943.

___ 6. "Go For Broke!" is called a pidgin English expression because
  a) it is a mixture of English and Hawaiian dialect.
  b) it is the standard language of the Hawaiian Islands.
  c) it is a slang phrase that originated in the mainland.

___ 7. During combat, Dan was shot in the stomach and lost
  a) his right leg.
  b) both arms.
  c) his right arm.

___ 8. After the war, Dan Inouye entered the University of Hawaii to study
  a) medicine.
  b) government and economics.
  c) business administration.

___ 9. When Hawaii was granted statehood, it became the
     a) forty-eighth state in the Union.
     b) forty-ninth state in the Union.
     c) fiftieth state in the Union.

___10. Dan Inouye's father was present when Dan was sworn into
     a) the House of Representatives.
     b) the Senate.
     c) both the House and the Senate.

___11. President John F. Kennedy invited Senator Daniel Inouye to the White House
     a) to have Dan meet other Senators.
     b) to appoint Dan to a committee.
     c) to meet Mr. Inouye, Dan's father.

___12. Senator Daniel Ken Inouye agreed to write *Journey to Washington,* his autobiography, so that there would be a record of his life for
     a) the people of Hawaii.
     b) his son.
     c) his wife, who helped him achieve his goal.

Can You Read a Bus Schedule?

Reading a bus schedule is easy, once you know how. Notice that the names of cities are listed in the center column. Arrival and departure times listed in heavy, dark type are for P.M.; times listed in light type are for A.M. An arrow indicates that the bus is non-stop, or an express bus. Unless there is a time listed for a city, the bus will not stop there. Some cities appear twice, which means that the bus has a stopover there. If you're going west, look at the columns on the left and read down. (For instance, if you are going from Omaha to Denver, Omaha appears *above* Denver in the center column, and you must read your schedule on the left-hand side.) If you're going east, look at the columns on the right and read up (for example, Kansas City to Chicago).

NEW YORK—CHICAGO/ST. LOUIS—DENVER

READ DOWN — **5** — **READ UP**

1-4-68

					Center (Lv / Ar)					
7 15	7 45	1 15	1 45	5 30	Lv New York, N.Y. ......(ET) **EGL**.. Ar	6 00	2 00	1045	7 30	7 00
9 40	3 15	3 15		7 30	Ar Philadelphia, Pa. Lv		1201			
1000		3 30		7 50	Lv Philadelphia, Pa. .... Ar		1130			
				1000	Lv Harrisburg .... Ar		9 20			
4 00	9 40			2 35	Ar Pittsburgh Lv		5 00			1145
4 35	1010			3 00	Lv Pittsburgh, Pa. .... Ar		4 35			1100
				1140	Ar Cleveland, O. Lv	8 15			8 30	
				1215	Lv Cleveland .... Ar	7 30			7 25	
					Lv Toledo, O. ......(ET)...... Ar				4 45	
1050		5 45			Ar Chicago, Ill. Lv	1201		6 00	1030	
1245		6 30			Lv Chicago, Ill. ......(CT) **CGL**.. Ar	1110		4 05	8 00	
		1025			Lv Davenport, Ia. .... Ar	4 45		1120	4 00	
6 35					Lv Cedar Rapids .... Ar					
9 45		3 05			Lv Des Moines, Ia. .... Ar	1256		6 55	1040	
1220		6 20			Ar Omaha, Neb. Lv	1000		4 20	7 45	
2 00		7 15			Lv Omaha, Neb. .... Ar	8 45		3 10	6 10	
7 55		1 45			Lv North Platte, Neb. Lv	1 35		9 45	1250	
9 20	2 35			8 50	Lv Columbus, O. ...... **EGL**.. Ar		1130			5 15
2 30	7 00			1 50	Lv Indianapolis, Ind. ......(ET)...... Ar		6 10			1 00
6 15		1115		5 45	Ar St. Louis, Mo. ......(CT)...... Ar		1201			6 45
5 55		1201		8 00	Lv St. Louis, Mo. ...... **CGL**.. Ar		1035			5 35
1010		2 42			Ar Columbia Lv		7 45			2 45
		3 38			Ar Boonville Lv		6 50			1 45
1250		5 30		1215	Ar Kansas City Lv		5 00			1145
1 45		6 40		1255	Lv Kansas City, Mo. .... Ar		3 40			1045
2 40		7 45		2 10	Ar Lawrence, Kan. Lv					9 45
3 18		8 20		2 40	Ar Topeka Lv		2 10			9 10
4 25		9 42		4 00	Ar Manhattan Lv		1245			7 45
5 00		1035		4 55	Ar Junction City Lv		1210			6 40
6 20		1140		6 01	Ar Salina Lv		1045			5 40
1208				1120	Ar Colby, Kan. ......(CT)...... Lv		5 45			
2 07		5 59		1 20	Ar Limon, Colo. ......(MT)...... Lv		1 40			9 20
4 15	3 30	8 20	5 55	3 10	Ar **DENVER** Lv	3 45	1130	12 01	6 30	7 15
4 15		8 30	7 15		Lv *Denver, CO* .... Ar	2 10	10 15	5 05	6 40	
			8 35		Ar *Colorado Springs, CO* Lv	12 50	11 20	8 55	4 45	
		5 20			Ar *Albuquerque, NM.* Lv	3 55		12 15	7 15	
		4 20			Ar *Phoenix, AZ* Lv	1 50		12 01	9 00	
		12 10			Ar *Los Angeles, CA* Lv	7 30		1 45	10 45	

Using the bus schedule on page 18, work the following exercises.

1. How many hours does it take a person to travel from New York to Chicago on the fastest bus? _____

2. What time would Mr. Green of Chicago leave if he is to meet his son for breakfast in North Platte at 9:00 A.M.? _____

3. At what time would Mrs. Carson reach Chicago if she left Denver by the bus that leaves nearest to noon? _____

4. Prepare a schedule for Mrs. Forbes of Los Angeles who is planning to visit her daughter in New York. She wishes to spend one night in Omaha, two nights in Chicago, and she wants to arrive in New York at 10:45 A.M.

Mrs. Forbes' Schedule

		DATE	TIME
Lv.	Los Angeles	May 1	_____
Ar.	Omaha	_____	_____
Lv.	Omaha	_____	_____
Ar.	Chicago	_____	_____
Lv.	Chicago	_____	_____
Ar.	New York	_____	_____

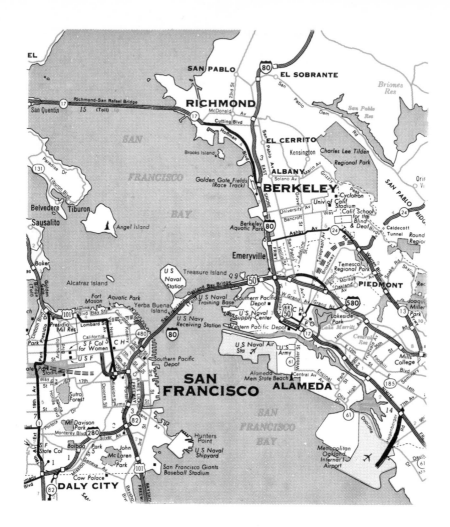

© Rand McNally & Co. R.L. 69-S-47.

Legend

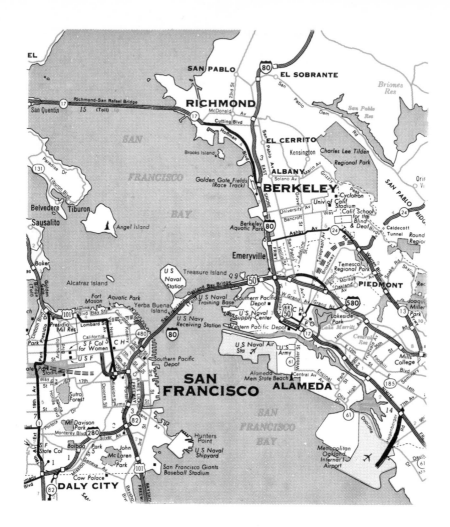 National interstate highway

U. S. highway

State highway

Airport

Reading a Road Map

Look at the map, carefully study the map legend, and then answer the questions.

1. What interstate highway would you use to travel between El Sobrante and Alameda? _____

2. Highway 24 between Ashby Avenue and the Caldecott Tunnel is classified as a _____

3. What bridge would you use to get from San Francisco to Emeryville? _____

4. What interstate route can you take from Berkeley to U.S. Highway 101? _____

5. How would you get from Richmond to Treasure Island (U.S. Naval Station)? _____

_____

_____

6. From El Sobrante you wish to go to the Oakland International Airport. What would be your most nearly direct route? _____

_____

_____

Would You Believe?

Many words in our language have fascinating stories. To know them is not only interesting, but gives us a better idea how our language has developed. Here are a few from this unit.

alarm
: **Definition:** sudden fear, warning sound
: **History:** This word came from the Italian *all' arme,* which meant "to arms." It was a cry to the people to pick up their weapons and defend themselves.

clue
: **Definition:** anything that serves to guide or direct in the solution of a problem
: **History:** In one of the Greek myths, Theseus used a ball of thread which he unwound to find his way out of a maze. The ball was called a *glauh* in Sanskrit; later it was called a *clew,* which is another way of spelling the word today.

infantry
: **Definition:** soldiers or military units that fight on foot
: **History:** The word comes from the Latin *infans,* which means "a youth." When knights were mounted on their horses, their knaves followed them on foot and were known as *infantis.* Since the knaves fought in battle, too, they became known as *foot soldiers.*

trivial
: **Definition:** of little importance, commonplace
: **History:** The Latin word *trivium* means a place where three roads meet (*tres,* three; *via,* way). That was the common place for meeting, and it was considered of little importance.

haggard
: **Definition:** wild-looking, untamed, hollow-eyed
: **History:** An Anglo-Saxon word, *haga,* meant "hedge." It was believed that witches were *hedge riders.* So witches became known as *hags,* and anyone who looked like a witch was called *haggard.*

sacrifice
: **Definition:** to give up at less than value
: **History:** At one time the word had only a religious meaning. Anything that was given either to the church or for one's own good was known as *sacrificium* (Latin), which came from two words—*sacer,* sacred; and *facere,* to make. Is a sacrifice play in baseball sacred today?

Analogies

A word analogy compares two sets of words. The first set has something in common. For instance, the set *anger: rage* has in common the fact that its two words have the same meaning. In order to complete the analogy, the words in the second set must also be alike as to meaning — *jail: prison*. The complete analogy, therefore, is *anger is to rage as jail is to prison*. To determine what analogy is used, you must discover how the words are *related*. Are they similar or opposite in meaning?

In the following exercises underline the word that best completes the analogy begun by the first set.

1. Night is to day as cold is to (frigid) (hot) (uncomfortable) (bright).

2. Real is to genuine as straight is to (crooked) (strong) (weak) (direct).

3. Look like is to resemble as famous is to (unknown) (celebrated) (mysterious) (wealthy).

4. Hateful is to detestable as birth is to (death) (beginning) (baby) (end).

5. Affirmative is to negative as asset is to (money) (income) (liability) (end).

6. Stimulate is to arouse as mourn is to (laugh) (grieve) (hate) (irritate).

7. Hazy is to clear as satisfaction is to (cheerfulness) (ridicule) (contentment) (discontentment).

8. Excuse is to forgive as hesitate is to (conceal) (expose) (pause) (run).

9. Exaggerate is to overstate as examine is to (guess) (pardon) (investigate) (release).

10. Courageous is to fearful as cheerfulness is to (sadness) (forgiveness) (charm) (punishment).

What's in Your Dictionary?

A dictionary contains much more than word definitions. Examine your own personal dictionary to see if it contains information like that listed below. The information may follow the regular alphabetical listing of the word it is associated with, but don't forget that many dictionaries have separate sections in the front and at the back for special kinds of facts.

Abbreviations: A good college dictionary will list common abbreviations. R.I.P. comes from the Latin, and means *rest in peace.* See if your dictionary tells you what S.R.O. means. _____

Places: Dictionaries often give information about mountains, cities, monuments, etc. Where are the Ryukyu Islands? _____

People: Biographical information will often be given about important people. Who was Modigliani? _____

Idioms: Common expressions used in English are usually listed under the most important word in the expression. What does *to double up* mean? _____

Synonyms and antonyms: Synonyms and antonyms are given after the regular definition. Give a synonym for *dogged.* _____

Prefixes and suffixes: Combining word parts are often defined. What does the suffix *-let* at the end of a word mean? _____

Trademarks: Popular trade names are also found in most dictionaries. Is *Levi's* a registered trademark? _____

Etymologies: The origin and history of many words are given. We can tell what language a word came from, when it first appeared in English, and its original spelling. From what language did the word *rhinoceros* come? _____

Colleges and universities: College dictionaries give data on the schools in the U.S. Can girls attend Rutgers University? _____

Parts Department: Negative Prefixes

A prefix is a group of letters added to the beginning of a word or root to change or to add to the meaning of the word or root. You can expand your knowledge of words by learning the meaning of the common prefixes.

Several prefixes mean *not*. These prefixes, which are called negative prefixes, are *un-, in-, im-, il-, ir-*.

Underline the negative prefix in each word.

1. immature
2. irregular
3. incapable
4. unlikely
5. illegal
6. impolite
7. illogical
8. improper
9. indirect
10. irreplaceable
11. impure
12. unbroken

Now say each of the words and instead of pronouncing the prefix, say *not*: For example, *not mature*. Do you get the meaning of the prefix?

Complete these sentences by writing the right word in the blank. Each word will contain a prefix that means *not*.

13. A person who is not active is _____.

14. A thing that is not balanced is _____.

15. An _____ schedule is not regular.

16. A man who is not employed is _____.

17. A person who is not literate is _____.

18. An article that is not expensive is _____.

19. When you are not comfortable, you are _____.

20. If you take a route that is not direct, it is an _____ route.

Underline the words that have prefixes that mean *not*. Remember to think about the meaning of each word. Not all the words contain negative prefixes.

1. impassable
2. important
3. unsteady
4. impress
5. illegible
6. immovable
7. improve
8. incorrect
9. increase
10. impatient
11. inaccurate
12. incident
13. uneven
14. indent
15. India
16. inconsiderate

17. illuminate	22. indefinite	27. insect	32. unsolved
18. industry	23. illustrate	28. irrigate	33. independent
19. irresistible	24. underhand	29. unlike	34. irrelevant
20. incomplete	25. impractical	30. irresponsible	35. illness
21. incurable	26. unjust	31. impossible	36. inexact

Sound Sense: Vowel Review

Underline the words that correctly complete these statements.

1. If the only vowel in a word or syllable is at the beginning or in the middle, the vowel is usually (short, long, silent). Write an example here:

2. If the only vowel in a word or syllable is at the end, the vowel is usually (short, long, silent). Write an example here: _____

3. When there are two vowels together in a word, one vowel usually stands for a (short, long) sound and the other vowel is (short, long, silent). Write an example here: _____

4. When two vowels appear in a word and one is a final e that is silent, the sound of the first vowel is usually (short, long, silent). Write an example here: _____

Mark the vowels in the words below. Put this mark ˘ over vowels that have a short sound; put this mark ¯ over vowels that have a long sound; and put this mark / through vowels that are silent. For example: dātę, făst.

5. mail	15. publish	25. discuss
6. jump	16. praise	26. incline
7. weave	17. untrod	27. grieve
8. throne	18. dismay	28. irate
9. gland	19. escape	29. release
10. glide	20. handbag	30. context
11. broke	21. prefixes	31. expose
12. locate	22. insane	32. athletic
13. intake	23. solid	33. bonfire
14. admit	24. claim	34. unite

So You Want a Job!

Your true pilot cares nothing about anything on earth but the river, and his pride in his occupation surpasses the pride of kings.

MARK TWAIN

From *Life on the Mississippi* by Mark Twain, Harper & Row, Publishers, Incorporated.

Key Words

<u>endure</u>–to undergo, bear; <u>congenial</u>–agreeable; <u>nutrition</u>–food; <u>chronic</u>–lasting a long time

Happiness Is a Good Job

William W. Bauer, M.D.

On the basis of a 40-hour week you spend just under one-quarter of your total time and about half your waking time on the job, except during vacations, illness, or unemployment. This should be a reasonably happy time, not a burden to be endured. Every effort should be made to find work that is congenial. Your job adjustment affects the health and happiness of you and your family.

The American Medical Association, in emphasizing the seven basic requirements for fitness, includes a good job among them. The other six are medical care, dental care, exercise and activity, good nutrition, rest and relaxation, and wholesome recreation.

What if you aren't happy in your job? There are several things you can do. You can relax and decide to let matters take their course. In that case, you may become a harmless and relatively useless drifter. You can grow into a chronic grouch to whom nothing is right in this worst of all possible worlds. (162 words)

Condensed from "How Do You Like Your Job?" *Today's Health*, published by the American Medical Association.

Talk It Over

1. How might the other six basic requirements for fitness affect a person on his job?
2. The author stated that several things could be done if you're not happy on the job. He listed only two. What would you do?

Key Words

priorities–coming before in order of importance; urgent–demanding immediate action

Where Will the Jobs Be?

The nation appears to be undergoing shifts in priorities, with more effort and funds heading for housing, pollution control, health care, transportation, and urban renewal, and lessened emphasis in such areas as military hardware, aerospace, and education. It makes oocupational needs more difficult to chart.

Such shifts have already altered the demand for some jobs that enjoyed strong growth in the 1960s. Teachers, for instance, have moved into a position of oversupply. And some 50,000 engineers are unemployed after an urgent need for their services during the sixties in aerospace and defense work. (93 words)

Talk It Over

1. What changes in our country have accounted for the shift in priorities for both jobs and money?

2. What changes in our society might account for the fact that we have an oversupply of teachers?

Sound Sense: Digraphs

When two consonants stand for a single sound, we have a *digraph*. Say these words to yourself and notice that the underlined letters stand for one sound.

choose	booth	machine	shot
what	these	graph	laugh

Underline the digraphs in these words.

1. lethal   3. chandelier 5. bother   7. which   9. phone
2. Michigan 4. push   6. shame   8. phase 10. enough

Sound Sense: Silent Consonants

In the many combinations of consonants we find in words, one of the letters may be silent. For example, in the word *write*, the *w* is silent. Cross out the silent consonant in each of these words:

1. dumb   4. wrist   7. walk

2. pneumonia   5. column   8. often

3. knob   6. gnat   9. palm

Sound Sense: Consonant Blends

Sometimes two consonants come together either at the beginning or at the ending of a word or syllable to form a combined sound called a *consonant blend*. Say these words, noting the sound made by the underlined consonants:

conf<u>l</u>i<u>ct</u>   fi<u>nd</u>   <u>sp</u>ider   <u>dr</u>aw   mi<u>ld</u>   su<u>pr</u>ise

Say each word below and listen for the blend. Underline the blend or blends in each word.

1. reflect   3. gland 5. closet 7. friend   9. decline   11. brush
2. hydroplane 4. spunk 6. draft   8. crisp   10. grandstand 12. slant

Sometimes three consonants form a blend, as in the word *splash*. Can you find the three-consonant blends in these words? Underline each one.

13. restrict   15. destroy   17. description   19. splendid
14. split   16. scrape   18. construct   20. sprinkle

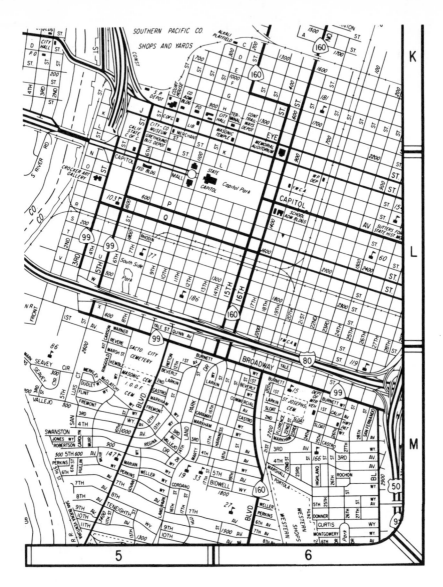

Index to Streets

Places of Interest

Can You Read a City Map?

One special kind of reading you are frequently called on to do is city-map reading. A city map tells you street names, locations of points of interest, distances between points, and most importantly, how to get from one point to another when traveling in the city.

See how good your map-reading skills are by answering these questions. Be sure to study the map key and index first.

1. The State Capitol Park is bounded by what four streets?

_____

2. If 12 blocks equal one mile, how far is it from the corner of 16th and E streets to 16th and Q?

_____

3. If you lived at the corner of Q Street and 9th, how would you get to Memorial Auditorium?

_____

_____

4. What would be the approximate address of the Y.W.C.A.?

_____

5. You have a bus to catch. You live on Broadway near Route 160. What would be the best route to the Greyhound Bus Depot?

_____

_____

_____

6. The State Capitol Building is in what direction from the Federal Building?

_____

7. Entering Sacramento from the west on Capitol Avenue, and staying on principal through-routes, map a route to Southside Park.

_____

_____

8. Looking for a job, you arrive at the Federal Building. You are referred to the School Administration Buildings. How far would you have to walk between these two locations?

_____

9. Plan an itinerary for a visitor to the places of interest in this city. Start the visitor as he enters the city from the north on Route 99. Give directions, street names, approximate addresses of locations, and approximate distances from one place to another.

_____

_____

_____

_____

_____

_____

_____

_____

_____

_____

Key Words
challenge–a demanding task; *merits*–worth, value

When to Quit

Many people simply don't know when to quit a job. They get a job, they stick with it, and they're stuck with it. Knowing when to quit a job that is either undesirable or lacking in challenge is just as important as knowing how to get a job.

A person should quit a job when he realizes that it is wrong for him. If he finds that he has to be a "yes man" in order to get ahead, he's in the wrong place. A man likes to get ahead because someone has recognized his merits and rewards his ideas.

If a job offers no training that will lead to a better position, it's the wrong job. A lifetime of no progress is a long time. The first ten years on a job should offer training for better things. The least a young person can expect from his first job is an opportunity to learn in order that he may improve both his skills and his chances for better pay. If the job offers no training, it's the wrong job for the man who wants to get ahead. (186 words)

True or False

Mark each statement either true (T) or false (F).
___ 1. On the whole, young people don't know when to quit jobs.
___ 2. When an employee becomes unhappy with his job, he should quit immediately.
___ 3. An employee should force himself to be a "yes man" and stay on the job.
___ 4. A good job should give the employee as much training as possible.
___ 5. A job should offer a chance for better skills and better pay.

Sound Sense: Consonant Review

Underline the consonant blends in these words.

1. thrash	6. fresh	11. scare	16. preface
2. splint	7. sponge	12. thrust	17. scale
3. fling	8. twine	13. prank	18. snake
4. space	9. gland	14. glance	19. triple
5. class	10. clue	15. planet	20. stale

Cross out the silent consonants in these words.

1. rhythm	6. whole	11. bridge	16. thought
2. answer	7. wretched	12. muscle	17. wreckage
3. listen	8. yacht	13. wring	18. rhapsody
4. watch	9. night	14. ghastly	19. mnemonics
5. mortgage	10. knock	15. isle	20. Rhine

Underline the digraphs in these words.

1. death	6. shield	11. chef	16. shift
2. whine	7. thorn	12. teach	17. digraph
3. typhoid	8. chore	13. bishop	18. whet
4. path	9. wheeze	14. chiffon	19. method
5. cough	10. beach	15. dolphin	20. nephew

Words You Need

Read each sentence and choose the meaning of the word in italics. Write the letter of your answer on the line. Use your dictionary if necessary.

___ 1. During the long storm, student *absenteeism* was high.
   Absenteeism means a) studying; b) anger; c) not being present.

___ 2. The speaker's *monotonous* voice began to put me to sleep.
   Monotonous means a) high pitched; b) loud; c) tiresome.

___ 3. The space agency is *abandoning* plans for further trips to the moon because it has no more money.
   Abandoning means a) continuing; b) giving up; c) making new.

___ 4. People were so unhappy with the new law that the senators set to work *humanizing* it more.
   Humanizing means a) reducing; b) increasing the power; c) making better for people.

___ 5. The dog *provoked* the cat into a fight.
   Provoked means a) scratched; b) stirred up; c) punished.

___ 6. The taste of the new ice cream was so rich that many people were *dissatisfied* with it.
   Dissatisfied means a) not pleased; b) happy; c) playing.

___ 7. The *ominous* note convinced them to pay the ransom for the return of their son.
   Ominous means a) ever present; b) threatening; c) beautiful.

___ 8. Color television sets are very complicated. It takes many workers to assemble their many *components*.
   Components means a) plugs; b) sizes; c) parts.

___ 9. Dr. Dixon's *affluence* made it possible for her to own a yacht and a private jet plane.
   Affluence means a) wealth; b) influence; c) freedom.

___10. Her *colleagues* at the office decided she was the most likely to become board president.
   Colleagues means a) friends; b) employees; c) fellow workers.

Beating Those Blue-collar Blues

Trevor Armbrister

At the Motorola plant near Fort Lauderdale, Fla., two dozen women formed an assembly line manufacturing tiny radio receivers. Each woman placed as many as ten parts on a printed circuit board, then passed the board to the person beside her. Absenteeism was high; so were turnover and product-quality complaints. At the end of the shift, employees raced one another to the door. "It was so monotonous," says 24-year-old Linda Thompson, "I'd go home ready to explode."

Then Motorola decided to produce a receiver with one third as many parts. Vice-president Martin Cooper had an inspiration. Why not let each worker build and test her own receiver? She could attach a note saying, "Dear Customer, I built this receiver and I'm proud of it. I hope it serves you well. Please tell me if it does not." Then she could sign her name and package the receiver herself. When individual assembly was introduced, absenteeism and turnover began to drop. So did customer complaints. "The key is involvement," Cooper says, beaming. "Abandoning the assembly line has produced people who *enjoy* their work."

Humanizing Jobs. Today, a wide range of employee-motivation experiments like this one are being tried across the country. Employers are realizing that people are capable of doing far more than their jobs either require or allow, that if they actually enjoy their work they will perform better. Work must not be simply the penalty that a person pays to survive; it must be something that offers meaning in and of itself. "Structuring jobs to be more meaningful and satisfying not only fulfills a social responsibility to those whom we employ," says Travelers Insurance Company's president M. H. Beach, "but it is good business as well."

Strategies vary from company to company, of course. Some firms—estimates range as high as 3,500—are adopting shorter work weeks or "gliding time" (in which employees pick the eight hours each day they'd prefer to work). Others are broadening the responsibility of individual jobs, giving workers more say about what they do and *how*. Still others are restructuring groups of jobs by creating work teams that set their own goals. "The idea," says Ed Dulworth, a General Foods plant manager in Topeka, Kan., "is to design work to fit people—not the other way around."

These strategies have provoked opposition from some labor unions and from management personnel basically distrustful of change and fearful of losing their authority. Yet in almost every case where they've been applied, they have increased productivity and reduced absenteeism and turnover rates. Already they have succeeded in motivating thousands of employees.

And clearly it's high time. A Gallup poll found that 13 percent of all workers are dissatisfied with their jobs. Two years later, that figure had jumped to 19 percent—and among workers between the ages of 18 and 29, to 33 percent. Absenteeism has reached as high as 15 percent at some auto plants on Mondays and Fridays—costing General Motors alone $50 million last year. Despite unemployment and a tight job market, turnover has increased. Drugs and alcohol are present on some assembly lines, and sabotage and acts of violence are on the rise.

Ominous Implications. Why do so many workers hate their jobs? Ironically, success has created the problem. For more than half a century, American business followed the theories of Prof. Frederick W. Taylor, father of scientific management. According to Taylor, the way to cut costs, increase volume, and realize maximum profits was to divide work into its smallest possible components, then rely on an assembly line where men could be trained to work like machines. If jobs were simple and repetitive, anyone could learn them quickly and perform them well. Parts were interchangeable—people were, too. "Above all," said Henry Ford in 1922, "the worker wants a job in which he does not have to think." Soon

America was transformed into a model of industrial efficiency, and American men and women were earning the highest wages any work force had ever received.

But the affluence that freed the average worker from strictly economic concerns also awakened his need for self-respect and fulfillment. Today's workers, better educated than those of any previous generation, have no interest in grinding factory routine or boring clerical tasks. They are less willing to submit to authority. They evaluate jobs in terms of personal satisfaction and the future. All too often, they conclude that there is no future.

The long-range implications of this malaise are ominous. For workers' attitudes toward their jobs will determine whether or not this country can meet intensifying foreign competition, and since 1965 the United States has had the worst productivity record of all the major powers. Traditional carrot-and-stick approaches will no longer check the trend. No matter how short the hours, how many the fringe benefits, or how high the pay, workers refuse to be treated like automatons.

The Team Concept. Not long ago, the University of Michigan's Survey Research Center asked 1533 employed persons which of 25 different job factors mattered most to them. "Interesting work" ranked first. "Good pay" was a distant fifth. Only if employees can find in their work a sense of achievement, recognition, responsibility, advancement, and personal growth will they be inspired to perform at capacity.

A team concept may prove to be the most successful and enduring of all the strategies companies are using to humanize work. Take the example of General Foods. At its new Gaines dog food plant in Topeka, workers are organized into processing, packaging and shipping, and office-duties teams. Each team member is encouraged to learn all the jobs his team performs, with his pay increasing as he learns. Once he masters all the jobs, he can move to another team—if his colleagues recommend him. Processing and packaging teams share responsibility for product quality and learn to test batches themselves. Teams meet at least once a week to discuss job assignments and operating or maintenance problems, and to interview and hire prospective employees when they are needed.

Technology has eliminated most of the dull, routine jobs in the new plant. Those that remain, General Foods executive Lyman D. Ketchum decided, would be rotated among *all* employees. There are no separate maintenance or utility departments. Each employee maintains his own equipment and cleans his own working space. Each is held accountable for his own mistakes.

Plant democracy goes even further: There are no executive dining rooms or reserved parking spaces. All employees come in through a single entrance. The carpeting on the floor of executive offices is identical to that in the workers' locker room. There are no time clocks or set hours for lunches and breaks.

Needed: A Joint Commitment. Despite the success of such approaches, job dissatisfaction won't disappear overnight. Some jobs are nonenrichable, and some workers just don't want more freedom and responsibility. What is needed is a joint commitment from both management and labor to seek new ways to better the quality of life on the job.

Management, now losing millions through absenteeism, turnover, sabotage, and drugs, should recognize that where jobs have been humanized, profits have increased. For their part, unions should realize that their members benefit when the rigidities of standard work practices are reduced and workers are challenged to greater productivity.

"There is no necessary conflict between doing right by people and financial success," General Foods' Ketchum points out. "But if you do *not* do right by your employees, their alienation could ultimately put you out of business." (1237 words)

Time:_____

Check It: Check the correct answer.

1. The main idea of this selection is that
___ a) people should be trained to work like machines.
___ b) workers are unhappy with their jobs.
___ c) it is possible to humanize blue-collar work while increasing productivity.

2. Motorola employees enjoyed their work more without

__ a) assembly lines.

__ b) interruptions.

__ c) extra work hours.

3. The practice of allowing workers to pick the eight hours each day they'd prefer to work is called

__ a) structuring jobs.

__ b) the carrot-and-stick approach.

__ c) gliding time.

4. Unions and management have been

__ a) opposed to change.

__ b) ignoring change.

__ c) in favor of change.

5. A Gallup poll found that workers' dissatisfaction is

__ a) increasing.

__ b) temporary.

__ c) less in the 18-to-29 age group.

6. "Above all, the worker wants a job in which he does not have to think," was said by

__ a) Henry Ford.

__ b) Professor Frederick Taylor.

__ c) a Gallup poll.

7. For today's workers the most important factor in evaluating jobs is

__ a) work hours.

__ b) personal satisfaction and the future.

__ c) fringe benefits and vacations.

8. Having groups of workers decide what work to do and when to do it is called

__ a) cooperative effort.

__ b) the team concept.

__ c) group discussion.

9. Eliminating executive dining rooms is an example of

___ a) employee action.

___ b) management concern.

___ c) plant democracy.

10. The author implies that, because of dissatisfaction, some workers are turning to

___ a) labor unions.

___ b) management.

___ c) drugs and alcohol.

Analogies

Analogies may show a relationship of a part to a whole. Example: hours : day — feet : yard. *Hours* is a part of a *day* as *feet* is a part of a *yard*. Still another analogy may show function. Example: pencil : writer — needle : seamstress. A *pencil* is used by a *writer* as a *needle* is used by a *seamstress*. In each of the following items underline the pair of words in parentheses which best matches the relationship of the first pair.

1. knob : door — (bicycle : pedal) (house : window) (page : book) (bed : sleep)
2. gills : breathing — (food : eating) (eyes : face) (ears : hearing) (fingers : hand)
3. one-half : one — (50 : 75) (25 : 50) (100 : 50) (10 : 5)
4. seamstress : pattern — (hammer : carpenter) (builder : blueprint) (books : student) (writer : reader)
5. mouth : face — (foot : toe) (word : sentence) (auto : tire) (body : waist)
6. rope : package — (tires : car) (binding : book) (flood : dam) (handle : knife)
7. wheel : hub — (apple : core) (clock : hand) (spoke : tire) (moon : beam)
8. Chicago : USA — (Paris : London) (Tokyo : Japan) (Europe : Germany) (Reno : Nevada)
9. fish : fin — (hat : head) (boat : oar) (air : breath) (wing : bird)

Job Application Forms

One of the most important things you do in applying for a job is filling out the application for employment form. The form represents you to your employer. He uses your completed form to get to know you. Often your answers to the questions on the form are the only means the employer has of deciding whether or not you can do the job.

Since the form is so important, it pays you to fill out the form correctly. It also pays to give some thought to the form before you actually start to fill it out. The forms on this page and the following pages are samples taken from actual employment applications.

General Information

All employment applications have space for general information about yourself: name, address, etc. If you are applying for a job in a defense industry or in the civil service, you may be required to supply security information. This helps the employer decide whether or not you can be trusted with confidential information.

APPLICATION FOR EMPLOYMENT

Position applied for _____ Date _____

Date available _____ Salary desired _____ Do you have reliable transportation? _____

If applying for part-time work, during what hours are you available? _____

If applying for temporary work, between what dates will you be available? _____
From   To

Name _____
         Last   First   Middle

Address _____ Telephone no. _____
         Number   Street   City   State   Zip

Are you under 18 or over 65? _____ Social sec. no. _____

Do you have any physical limitations? If so, describe _____

Have you had any major illness in the past 5 years? If so, describe _____

44

Previous Experience

One of the most important areas that the prospective employer is interested in is that of previous experience. Note again the types of questions asked, and therefore the types of information you must have at your fingertips. Note also the order: You are to list your present or most recent job first and work backward to other positions.

EMPLOYMENT RECORD

Please account for all employed time during, but not limited to, the past four years. List your most recent position first:

Name of
employer _____ Tel. no. _____

Kind of
Address _____ business _____
        Number   Street   City   State   Zip

Name and title
of supervisor _____

Title of your   Employment   Salary at
position _____ dates: From _____ To _____ termination _____

Description of
work performed _____
_____
_____

Reason for
leaving _____

Name of
employer _____ Tel. no. _____

Kind of
Address _____ business _____
        Number   Street   City   State   Zip

Name and title
of supervisor _____

Title of your   Employment   Salary at
position _____ dates: From _____ To _____ termination _____

Description of
work performed _____
_____

Reason for
leaving _____

References and Education

Most employers will check with other people who have hired you, to find out how good a worker you are. They may even check on your ability to make friends and to get along with people. For this reason, employment applications often have a section asking for personal and/or professional references. It is important here to list people's names who have knowledge of your personal characteristics.

Your prospective employer will also require information about your education—particularly that which might have prepared you for the job you have in mind. Notice that you are required to begin with your high school education. Dates of attendance, subjects taken, and grade-point average are required. It often pays to have this information written down prior to filling out the form.

Character References   (Please list three business or professional people who are not related to you)

Name	Address	Tel. no.	Position

EDUCATION

High
school _____ Location _____

    Year   Course of
    graduated _____ study _____

College 1. _____ Location _____

    No. of   Year
    years ____ graduated ____ Degree _____ Major _____ Minor _____ G.P.A. ____

    2. _____ Location _____

    No. of   Year
    years ____ graduated ____ Degree _____ Major _____ Minor _____ G.P.A. ____

Other degrees: Area of
College _____ Degree _____ specialization _____

Scholarships, honors,
extracurricular activities _____

Other education
(Include military service schools) _____

Parts Department: Prefixes

A prefix is a group of letters added to the beginning of a word or a root form to change the meaning or to add to the meaning of the word or root. Knowing the meaning of many prefixes will help you to understand the meaning of many words. Here are some common prefixes and their meanings. Study them carefully.

re- This prefix has two meanings. It may mean "back," as in return or retain. Or, it may mean "again," as in reapply or replay.

pre- Means "before," as in predict and premature. (*Prelude* and *preplay* mean the same thing. *Prelude* comes from the Latin *prae*, before, and *ludere*, to play.)

per- This prefix means "through," as in perfume (from the Latin *per*, through, and *fumare*, smoke). How do you suppose *perfume* came to mean what it does today?

de- Means "away from" or "do the opposite of," as in deport and demobilize.

ex- You may use this prefix frequently to mean "out of," "from," or "former," as in export, extract, or ex-president.

mis- This prefix may mean "bad," "badly," "wrongly," as in misinformation, mispronounced, or mistaken.

dis- "Opposite of" or "away" are meanings of this prefix, as in discomfort or dismiss.

Write one of these prefixes to complete the meaning of the sentences.

    re-   pre-   per-   de-   ex-   mis-   dis-

1. She had to ____frost her refrigerator.

2. Everyone seems to ____agree with me.

3. Last night they saw a ____view of a movie.

4. Be careful not to ____spell that word.

5. You will need a ____mit to enter the building.

6. The wall ____tended into the garden.

7. She couldn't ____call his name.

Words You Need

Read each sentence and choose the meaning of the word in italics. Write the letter of your answer on the line. Use your dictionary if necessary.

___ 1. Rob told his *prospective* partner about the kind of company he would be joining.

a) previous; b) enthusiastic; c) expected

___ 2. The statement from the defense department was very *concise;* it contained fewer than 25 words.

a) brief; b) severe; c) demanding

___ 3. His speech contained a great deal of information not directly related to the topic: the *irrelevant* facts spoiled the presentation.

a) important; b) uninteresting; c) inapplicable

___ 4. The chairman was so *overbearing* he wouldn't allow anyone else to speak at the meeting.

a) domineering; b) talkative; c) excited

___ 5. During the question-and-answer period, the blonde asked the lecturer the *inane* question, "What time is it?"

a) important; b) brief; c) meaningless

___ 6. Amy is known for her *punctuality;* she's never late for an appointment.

a) promptness; b) reliability; c) sharpness

___ 7. Bob and Larry are *veteran* campers; they've made six camping trips to the Sierra.

a) warlike; b) experienced; c) brave

___ 8. Shaking your head is *equivalent* to saying "no."

a) emphasis; b) the opposite of; c) equal

Big Job of Job Hunting

Some people tend to look upon job hunting as an enormous hurdle and an unpleasant struggle — a task perhaps comparable to scaling Mount Everest on an empty stomach. The effort takes preparation and the know-how to handle the "terrain." And the reward at the end of the path is well worth the effort.

Before you begin your assault of "Mount Job," get some idea of the direction you will take. What kind of work can you do? What would you like to do? Your decision need not be rigid, for you may have to change your approach as you go along. But if you have a rough idea of where you are headed, this could save you from having to make some unnecessary "detours" later along the way.

Now, how do you find jobs? One way is to talk to friends and relatives who might provide you with valuable contacts. But in most cases contacts provide only an opening wedge. In the end you must still sell yourself to the prospective employer on your own merits.

Your teacher or guidance counselor might also be able to help you in seeking out prospective employers. A recommendation from your school will certainly add weight to your application for employment.

Here are some other starting points:

Want Ads: In metropolitan areas, check the classified "want ads" in your daily or weekly newspaper. This may lead you to a specific job opening. If not, it will at least give you some over-all view of job opportunities in your area, the qualifications required for certain jobs, and in some cases the salaries that you might reasonably expect from an employer as well.

Employment Agencies: In visiting employment agencies, remember that there are two basic types—private and public. Private agencies often have job listings that are unavailable anywhere else. But if a private agency succeeds in placing you in a job, it will charge a fee for its services (unless the employer agrees to pay the fee). Public employment agencies are operated by federal, state, and local governments and they usually do not charge for their services. Public agencies are particularly good spots for jobs having any connection with civil service. Remember that most public and some private employment agencies offer testing programs and other counseling aid to help you decide on a career.

Making the Rounds: A direct approach is simply to visit the companies and factories in your area. A neat, well-written letter of inquiry to the company's employment or personnel department could be the starter. It is highly advisable to telephone the personnel director to make an appointment instead of just "dropping in."

Regardless of the type of job you are seeking, your chances of landing it depend greatly on how well you present yourself and your qualifications. Some of this presentation may come through the written word—letters, filling out forms, and so on. Some of it is a personal presentation which may come in a personal interview.

Let's take the written presentation first. If you intend to write a letter of application, make it neat, follow the business letter form, and watch your spelling! Write in your own style and try to keep it brief—no more than a typewritten page at the most.

The purpose of the letter is to get the prospective employer interested in you right off the bat. Tell him what type of job you are seeking and what kind of employee you expect to be. In short, give him some idea why he should be interested in you.

Include with the letter an outline of your qualifications— an outline that usually goes under the name of résumé (that's pronounced REH-zoo-may). The résumé must include such vital statistics as date of birth, age, height, state of health, home address and telephone number, and so on. It should also list your previous job experiences (in reverse chronological order—that is, list your most recent job first and then work backward), your education, and such things as related hobbies and interests.

You should also include in your résumé the names and addresses of at least two persons who will serve as personal references. In most cases these references should be adults but not relatives. Your teacher, your priest, pastor, or rabbi, or former employers are among those who might serve as references. It is both wise and courteous to get their permission.before listing them as your references.

Again, be complete and specific (use descriptive job titles, specific addresses)—but be as concise as possible. Busy executives do not have the time—and may not have the will—to wade through a 30-page epic of your life. Organize your information and eliminate anything that is obvious or irrelevant.

Once your groundwork is completed, the day comes when you receive a letter or a call setting an appointment for a personal interview. In the course of your job hunting, you'll probably have several interviews. This is a critical phase in getting a job—and you'll want to make the best impression you can.

There's a saying, "You can't tell a book by its cover." But don't take this expression too much to heart. People can tell a lot about a person from his appearance. Your best guide in dressing for an interview is: try to wear the type of clothing which best suits the job you are seeking. For instance, it would be unwise to approach an interview for a banking position wearing loud sports clothing.

Before you go to the interview, make sure you have all the facts and data about yourself straight. You may be asked to fill out standard application forms—and some of those exact names, dates, addresses, and social security numbers (if you have one) are not easy to remember. If you can keep all those data in your head, good. If not, write them down somewhere and keep the information handy. This is one place where an extra copy of your résumé might come to the rescue.

Also, if at all possible, learn something about the company you are about to visit. You do not make a very good impression if you find yourself asking the interviewer such questions as: "And what does your company do?"

Now that you are all dressed up with someplace to go — get there on time! Being late for the interview will make the interviewer wonder about your everyday punctuality.

When invited into the office, walk in confidently and greet the interviewer in a natural voice, neither mumbling nor shouting. Let him be the one to offer to shake hands. His invitation to sit down is not an invitation to slouch. Remember your posture. Your attitude toward the job is revealed in the way you sit, listen, and talk (with as much confidence as possible without being overbearing).

Remember that while the company that is interviewing you has something to offer you, you also have something to offer the company — your services. Don't sell yourself short. You should have in mind all the experience and knowledge you've acquired that can be applied to the job. Bragging, of course, is not going to help you a bit. But you shouldn't be too humble either.

Be prepared to answer questions about your interests and your long-range plans. The interviewer will probably give you all the necessary information about salary, hours, vacation policies, and so on. But if you have additional questions, don't hesitate to ask them. In fact, good questions are an excellent way of presenting yourself. However, don't ask such inane questions as: "How long are the coffee breaks around here?"

If the interviewer mentions a specific salary, fine — you have your choice of accepting or not. If he doesn't and throws the ball to you, you may be in for a tricky moment. What figure should you mention?

In your pre-interview preparations, you may have gotten some idea of the pay range of the job you are seeking. Set a range for yourself and, in the words of veterans in the employment field, "Ask for the higher figure but be prepared to settle for the lower." Salary is important, of course, but don't overdo it. Instead, emphasize your interest in the job and hopes for advancement rather than your starting pay. Most companies like ambitious employees — not grasping ones.

When the interview is over, rise, thank the interviewer cordially, and leave. If he says, "We'll call you," or the equivalent, it's a good idea to write a follow-up letter thanking him and reminding him of your interest. This can't hurt — and may help by showing him the seriousness of your purpose.

As one executive of an international corporation once said, "Getting the job is the hardest job of all." But that does not mean you can sit back and relax. Once you have hurdled the big job hunt, you will want not only to keep your job but to advance in it as well. A willingness to learn and improve your skills is important. If you approach your job with the same thoughtfulness and dedication that you showed in finding it, you'll do just fine. (1524 words)

Time:_____

True or False

Mark each statement either true (T) or false (F).

___ 1. The main idea of this selection is that the process of job hunting should not be taken lightly.

___ 2. Relatives, friends, teachers, and counselors are often helpful in seeking prospective employers.

___ 3. An overall view of job opportunities in your area can be obtained in the classified section of your newspaper.

___ 4. Public and private employment agencies have identical listings.

___ 5. Just dropping in on the personnel director is an advisable technique.

___ 6. Your presentation of yourself is the ultimate thing that will decide whether or not you get the job.

___ 7. The longer your résumé is, the more impressed your prospective employer will be.

___ 8. You need to do some preparation before the interview.

Talk It Over: The author discusses behavior and appearance during an interview. Is he indicating that you should not be an individual? How are you going to stand out from other applicants?

Parts Department: Prefix Review

Write the meaning of each underlined prefix.

1. To <u>re</u>pay someone is to pay _____.

2. A word that is <u>mis</u>pronounced is pronounced _____.

3. Food that has been <u>pre</u>cooked has been cooked _____.

4. If you <u>re</u>read a sentence, you are reading it _____.

5. <u>Dis</u>satisfied is the _____ satisfied.

6. To make <u>per</u>forations on paper is to make holes _____ it.

7. To <u>de</u>port someone from this country is to send him _____ it.

8. To <u>ex</u>haust stale air from a room is to draw the air _____ it.

9. To <u>dis</u>miss students is to send them _____.

10. To <u>re</u>turn something is to give it _____.

11. <u>Dis</u>like is the _____ like.

12. <u>Mis</u>understand is to understand _____.

13. <u>Re</u>write is to write _____.

14. <u>Pre</u>fix means to fix or to place something _____.

15. <u>De</u>grade means to take an honor or rank _____ someone.

16. <u>Dis</u>continue means the _____ _____ continue.

17. <u>Dis</u>pense means to give _____.

18. To <u>ex</u>tract a tooth is to pull it _____ someone's mouth.

54

Use and Abuse

The desire to take medicine is perhaps the greatest feature that distinguishes man from animals.

Sɪʀ Wɪʟʟɪᴀᴍ Oꜱʟᴇʀ

Key Words

organism–any living thing; *toxin*–poisonous product of animals or plants; *repulse*–drive back; *averted*–prevented from happening

Miracle Drugs

Fred Reinfield

The best known of the miracle drugs are the antibiotics, but there are other and newer types. The antibiotic substances, produced by living organisms (mostly molds) have the power to kill or check the growth of bacteria. The job of the antibiotics generally is to aid the white blood cells by stopping the bacteria from multiplying.

When a person is killed by a disease, it means that the bacteria have multiplied faster than the white blood cells could devour them, and that the bacterial toxins increased more rapidly than the antibodies could neutralize them. The help that the antibiotics give the white blood cells and antibodies is generally enough to repulse an attack of the germs.

Before the use of antibiotics, many patients recovered through the strength of their natural defenses. But with the introduction of the antibiotics, the proportion of fatalities has been greatly decreased; the length and severity of illness have been cut down considerably; and many harmful and painful side effects of disease have been averted. (169 words)

True or False

Mark each statement either true (T) or false (F).

___ 1. The antibiotics are the newest type of miracle drugs.
___ 2. When a person is killed by a disease, it means that white blood cells have multiplied faster than bacteria.
___ 3. Antibiotics are produced from non-living organisms, such as molds.

_____ 4. Since the introduction of antibiotics, fatalities have decreased.

_____ 5. Harmful and painful side effects of disease have been increased through the use of miracle drugs.

Sound Sense: Long Vowel Sounds

i before *ld* in a word usually stands for the long sound: mild, child, wild.

o before *ld* in a word usually stands for the long sound: cold, mold, sold.

i before *nd* in a word usually stands for the long sound: mind, grind, find. (But the *i* stands for both the long and short sounds in *wind!*)

i before *gh* or *ght* in a word usually stands for the long sound: sigh, night, light, high.

oo may stand for several sounds: moon, good, floor, blood, brooch.

Analogies

Analogies may show cause and effect. Example: sadness may lead to tears—search may lead to discovery. Still another analogy may show a symbolic relationship. Example: lion is a symbol of monarchy—owl is the symbol of wisdom. In each of the following items underline the word that best completes the analogy. Use your dictionary if necessary.

1. haste : blunder—joke : (pun) (comedy) (laughter) (tragedy)

2. thrift : savings—effort : (failure) (achievement) (study) (work)

3. suspicion : distrust—anguish : (hope) (drive) (misery) (goal)

4. symptom : disease—pain : (doctor) (nurse) (medicine) (discomfort)

5. failure : disappointment—cyclone : (wind) (rain) (destruction) (cold)

6. white : purity—red : (color) (heat) (danger) (light)

7. USA : eagle—England : (bear) (falcon) (lion) (serpent)

8. Illinois : Land of Lincoln—California : (Centennial State) (Lone Star State) (Evergreen State) (Golden State)

9. vanity : peacock—innocence : (bluebird) (cub) (hawk) (lamb)

10. dove: peace — elephant: (Republican Party) (Democratic Party) (Freedom Party) (Communist Party)

11. snake: deceit — oak: (acorn) (height) (age) (strength)

Key Words

psyche–the mind; *alleviating*–making easier to bear; *mania*–a form of mental disorder; *indiscriminate*–not based on careful choice

Our Pill-filled Lives

Headache? Take a pill. Depressed, tense? Take a pill. Runny nose, arthritis, heart pain, stomach-ache – pills, pills, pills. And so it goes. Millions of Americans take pills on their own or on their doctors' say-so every day for every ill from an upset stomach to an upset psyche. We consume tons of drugs at a cost of almost $4,000,000,000 each year. An obvious result of all this pill-taking has been the alleviating of much suffering and the saving of many lives.

Now, however, many thoughtful leaders of the United States medical profession are having second thoughts about America's – and the world's – pill mania. They see a coming epidemic of pill-caused diseases. They worry about the silent and possibly deadly effects of long-term pill-taking. They fear that lifesaving pills can lose their power through indiscriminate use. They even suspect that many medicines now prescribed have no beneficial effects at all. And they look with horror at the tendency of some physicians to overprescribe and the tendency of many patients to demand and often obtain unneeded and even dangerous drugs. (178 words)

From *The World Book Year Book.* © 1967 Field Enterprises Educational Corporation.

Check It

Write the letter of the correct answer on the line.

___ 1. In the sentence, "An obvious result of all this pill-taking has been the alleviating of much suffering," the word *alleviating* means

    a) deepening.   b) extension.   c) relief.

___ 2. In the sentence, "They fear that lifesaving pills can lose their power through indiscriminate use," the word *indiscriminate* means

a) careful.   b) careless.   c) dangerous.

Parts Department: Plurals

When s or es is added to a word to show that it means more than one, the word is then *plural*. Most words are made plural by adding s: kites, boys, things, papers, walls.

Say these words and notice carefully how each one ends: church(es), class(es), bush(es), fox(es), fuzz(es). What is the difference between the plurals of these words and the words in the paragraph above?

1. Complete this statement about plurals: When words end in s, x, z, ch, or sh, their plurals are formed by adding _____ .

Now, make each of these words plural by adding either s or es:

2. wish____   4. tax____   6. room____   8. ash____
3. vase____   5. word____   7. peach____   9. breeze____

Look at the words in Row 1. Each word ends in y. Now look at the plural form of each word in the second row.

ROW 1:   baby   chimney   lady   key   toy
ROW 2:   babies   chimneys   ladies   keys   toys

10. Note the letter that comes before the y in each of the words in the first row, and complete this statement: When there is a vowel before a final y, the plural is formed by adding _____ ; when there is a consonant before a final y, the y is changed to _____ and the plural is formed by adding _____ .

Write the plurals for each of the following words.

11. candy   12. highway   13. pulley   14. pantry   15. tray

_____   _____   _____   _____   _____

Some words change their spelling to show that they stand for more than one thing. For example: man, men; mouse, mice; foot, feet; woman, women; tooth, teeth; goose, geese.

Key Words
supplement–something added to complete a thing or make it better;
bombarded–attacked; *illusion*–a false idea

Vitamin Overdose

Overdose on vitamins? Experts agree that most vitamin overdoses don't do any harm; they are merely turned into waste by the body. However, kidney damage can result from too much vitamin D, and more than 50,000 units of vitamin A daily can result in severe disorders of the nervous system, bones, and other tissues. Research which could tell us about the effects of excessive amounts of vitamins over long periods of time has not been done.

Advertisements by drug companies and health food advocates have made the public very aware of vitamins. We are bombarded with vitamin information on TV, billboards, and in magazines. The public is under the illusion that vitamins insure good nutrition. Consumers Union, the nonprofit organization that publishes *Consumer Reports*, states that the public would be better off if the $400 million spent annually on vitamins were left in bank accounts.

Nutritionists believe that healthy people who eat proper amounts of meat, eggs, milk products, fruits, vegetables, breads and other cereal products do not need vitamin supplements. There is no substitute for eating right. But many perfectly normal people who are getting all they need from balanced diets are still going to continue buying vitamins just for the emotional satisfaction.

Talk It Over

1. Why do people take vitamins even though they have a balanced diet?

2. What limitations should there be on vitamin ads?

Words You Need

Read each sentence and choose the meaning of the word in italics. Write the letter of your answer on the line. Use your dictionary if necessary.

___ 1. Because so many children were suffering from it, the flu *contagion* began to worry health officials.

    Contagion means a) the excitement of the times; b) the spreading of a disease; c) the continuation of hatred.

___ 2. He lived under the *stigma* of having been in prison.

    Stigma means a) something which aids movement in social groups; b) something which gives high social status; c) something which is considered shameful.

___ 3. Men and women suffering from a variety of *psychoses* were placed in the state's mental hospital for treatment.

    Psychoses are a) forms of mental disorder; b) medical students; c) physical ailments.

___ 4. The grand jury formally *indicted* the arrested man for murder; his trial will begin next week.

    Indicted means a) jailed; b) cleared; c) accused.

___ 5. The woman started *insidious* rumors and succeeded in turning the neighbors against Miss Polk.

    Insidious means a) secretly harmful; b) constructive; c) humorous.

___ 6. Motorists who drive below the speed limit on freeways are a *menace* to the safety of others.

    Menace means a) threat; b) bore; c) aggravation.

___ 7. We had many *discordant* views expressed in our discussion group today—there was no agreement.

    Discordant means a) agreeable; b) disorderly; c) not in agreement.

___ 8. A good leader has a *composite* of many important traits, such as gentleness, kindness, moral strength, and a sense of humor.

    Composite means a) promise; b) goodness; c) combination.

Why Americans Hide Behind a Chemical Curtain

Roland H. Berg

An epidemic of drug abuse is sweeping the nation. The contagion, centered on college campuses, also infects high school students and adults in our cities, suburbs, and small towns. No one is immune.

We are a drug-dependent society. At its peak is the small, perhaps diminishing, group of narcotic addicts: urban, poor. At its base are the millions of Americans who can't sleep, wake up, or feel comfortable without drugs. Most of these are white and wealthy. The kids smoke marijuana and pop in hallucinogens; the parents swallow medicines that may be needless, self-prescribed, or harmful; barbiturates, amphetamines, laxatives, pain-killers, and tummy soothers. They don't know—or won't admit—they are "hooked" on drugs. Their habits create no social stigma. With the exception of marijuana, STP, and LSD, their drugs have accepted medicinal uses and can be found in most bathroom cabinets. The trouble lies not in the pills, but in the people.

Drugs are no longer only a slum problem. Some experts even feel that addiction among people living in the hope-killing ghettos is decreasing. They see them rejecting the heroin retreat, not wanting to stay where they are, but getting out. Heroin boxes them in.

Meanwhile, serious drug problems sweep through white America: Junction City, Kans.; Pagedale, Mo.; Woodford, Va.; Plymouth, Mich.—places with apple-pie smells and wind-snapped flags. No one knows how many middle-class Americans are involved. Police officials estimate that between 15 and

50 percent of the teen-agers in *any* suburban community may be experimenting with marijuana. However, adults may be the biggest drug users, a fact hard to check and easy to hide. Police and doctors dislike reporting the activities of the leaders of their communities.

Who are the wealthy drug takers? They are the 30-year-old architect in Atlanta who drank and took pills and now can't work. Or the construction engineer who got into debt and took pills for two years to calm his nerves. He can't stop. Or the insurance salesman who drank all the time, and his wife thought the big thing to do was take pills and get high with him. Or the Detroit, Mich., lawyer who took amphetamines to keep him alert through a tough real-estate problem that lasted several weeks. He couldn't stop taking them. He had to use barbiturates to sleep. Over a two-year span of increasing dependence, he couldn't appear in court or work, he was not allowed to practice law, his marriage fell apart.

Middle-class people are afraid to admit they depend on drugs. Although they are using pills, many may not realize they've got a problem. Some may not even know they are taking them.

These middle-class drug users live in a chemical world that may be more dangerous and harder to escape than their old one. Barbiturates, hallucinogens, amphetamines and certain tranquilizers are dangerous.

Essentially, all drugs are harmful. Even when used medically, they do their good deeds by unnaturally altering the function or chemical structure of various organs in the body. A physician weighs carefully possible harm against possible good. The nonmedical, unsupervised use of drugs holds no safeguards, only dangers.

LSD is a case in point. More and more users, taking LSD in city apartments and off-campus houses, are ending up in hospitals with psychoses. Early, inconclusive reports indicate that LSD may also damage chromosomes—the cells that dictate our inherited characteristics. Hard-core acid heads are injecting LSD into their veins—main-lining—for a faster high (the drug takes 15 to 45 minutes when swallowed). They are suffering the needle-induced diseases of the heroin and amphetamine main-liner: local abscesses, phlebitis, hepatitis, endocarditis and pulmonic foreign-body reactions.

A new, more powerful drug, STP, has appeared in Greenwich Village, San Francisco, and San Bernardino, Orange, and Riverside counties in California. At least 12 persons have been hospitalized after swallowing blue-spotted, white STP capsules. The drug, dubbed a "mega-hallucinogen," takes a user on a three-to-four-day drug "trip." (LSD lasts eight to twelve hours.) There are two dangers already known about STP: 1) it may cause atropine poisoning, with respiratory paralysis; 2) the tranquilizer chlorpromazine, used to calm down LSD "trippers," can't be taken because it heightens the effects of STP. The letters may come from a motor-fuel additive named STP, which means scientifically treated petroleum.

The case against marijuana isn't clear. Many authorities testify that smoking pot is no more injurious than smoking tobacco—which is not without harm. Physiologically, that's true. Marijuana has been wrongfully indicted as a narcotic.

The hang-up on stimulants, depressants, and tranquilizers often begins with the physician prescribing the drug for a real medical need. The dangers grow from there. Tranquilizers and amphetamines may induce psychic or emotional dependence. Amphetamines stimulate a feeling of well-being. They pep you up; but they can also cause permanent, organic brain damage or serious psychiatric disorders.

Barbiturates are depressants that help in illness and insomnia. But abused—as they are on a large scale—they have become a major drug menace. Heavy use makes a person stagger, slur his speech, become uncoordinated. An excess can paralyze the breathing center of the brain and cause death. Each year, some 3,000 Americans take a fatal dose, many accidentally. Barbiturates lead all other drugs as a cause of death.

It is easy to take an overdose. The drug confuses thinking, and the body builds tolerance, requiring larger and more dangerous doses to achieve the desired effect. The heavy barbiturate user will suffer the agonies of withdrawal, usually far more dangerous than a narcotic addict's. Barbiturate withdrawal, unless under a physician's supervision, may take as long as three weeks and can result in convulsions and death.

Why do we take these drugs? The pressures and demands of society may become too much for adults to bear. They may have family and job problems and anxieties, the feeling of being trapped by split-level existence. They find artificial ways to escape from hard realities. "But more than this," says Dr. Fox, "they are unable to adjust to middle-class adulthood — its mores, hang-ups, and pressures. They escape into drugs. This is the insidious kind of thing: They take pills to sleep and pills to stay awake, pills to calm down and pep up. They take drugs to keep going through life."

College and high-school kids are different. They are just starting life. Why do they take drugs?

Dr. Kenneth Keniston, associate professor of psychiatry at Yale University, goes beyond the pat explanations — rebellion, kick, etc. — to add a new theory. At a Drug Education Conference held in Washington, D.C., he claimed that today's youths who seek an answer to the traditional cry, "Who am I?" face special problems that yesterday's adolescents didn't confront.

Dr. Keniston believes it takes more knowledge to get ahead nowadays, and modern youth is crawling into an inner shell to avoid being overstimulated by the discordant sights and sounds of modern living. The here and now, Dr. Keniston says, have become overly important.

Research psychologist Richard H. Blum, at Stanford University's Institute for the Study of Human Problems, went to the source to learn who takes drugs and why. Dr. Blum and his associates interviewed at random 200 persons, young and old, living in the San Francisco Bay Area. Their interviews painted a revealing composite of the kind of people who are heavy drug users.

They are more often white than Negro, and they are better educated, divorced more often, earn more money, and have fewer political ties than the average person. Also, they rebel against authority and frequently express dislike of their parents, themselves, and their work. Heavy users reveal strong likes and dislikes, are compulsive about their activities and show numerous signs of inner conflicts. They use drugs for religious motives or for self-analysis. As a group, they told of frequent use of medicinal drugs during childhood.

Dr. Blum concludes that those students and adults who turn to LSD, marijuana, and pills are "inner" people; those who do not abuse drugs, he calls the "outer" people. Inner people concentrate on the thoughts that swirl within their heads. Outer people look to external experiences, what's happening around them.

Contrary to claims of indescribable delights by some drug takers, most people use drugs to relieve anxiety. They're not pursuing pleasure, they just hurt less on drugs. This is true also of hard-narcotic users. A heroin addict told a reporter, "You don't even know what I'm talking about; you feel okay all the time. Me, it costs me $100 a day just to stop hurting so much."

Fundamentally, drug abuse is a health and social problem, not a police problem. Stopping the hurt isn't easy. The solution is education, not punishment. We are a pill-oriented society, conditioned to find happiness through chemistry. If any "crash" program is needed, it should call for more knowledge and understanding of the role of drugs. It should focus on the kids who are trying drugs today on college campuses and in hippy hangouts. They have the most to lose from drug abuse.

We must make the outside world more attractive than the inner. Arresting people and putting them behind bars is no better than letting them hide behind a chemical curtain. Either way, they are in prison. (1529 words)

Time:_____

Check It

Check the correct answer.

1. The main idea of this selection is that

___ a) drug addiction is a serious problem only in slums.

___ b) we must make the outside world more attractive.

___ c) almost all drugs are harmful in one way or another.

2. The problem of drug addiction lies in the
___ a) needs of people.
___ b) availability of drugs.
___ c) variety of drugs.

3. People in the slum areas seem to be turning away from drugs
___ a) because they want to stay in the ghetto.
___ b) because they don't like the taste of drugs.
___ c) because drugs keep them in the ghetto.

4. The biggest drug abusers may be
___ a) teen-agers.
___ b) adults.
___ c) middle-aged women.

5. The danger of marijuana is that it may
___ a) be a narcotic.
___ b) be more harmful than tobacco.
___ c) like tobacco, be harmful to your health.

6. Adults take drugs because
___ a) of the hard realities of living.
___ b) of the enjoyment of the act.
___ c) of their families.

7. According to Dr. Keniston, youths take drugs to keep from being
___ a) examined by others.
___ b) socially unpopular.
___ c) overstimulated by modern living.

8. The author tries to get across the idea that drugs
___ a) should never be used.
___ b) keep people isolated from others.
___ c) are of no value medically.

Talk It Over

The title of this selection uses the term "chemical curtain." How does drug abuse resemble a curtain?

Parts Department: Prefix Review

Write the meaning of each underlined prefix.

1. <u>Pre</u>historic people lived _____ history was recorded.

2. The cook was <u>dis</u>missed; he was sent _____.

3. An <u>un</u>reliable person is _____ reliable.

4. An <u>ex</u>cavator is a machine that digs holes or hollows _____ dirt.

5. To <u>de</u>hydrate vegetables means to take water _____ them.

6. Because the cave was <u>in</u>accessible, we could _____ get in.

7. When someone <u>re</u>applies for a job, he is applying _____.

8. <u>Mis</u>directions are _____ directions.

9. A <u>re</u>porter is one who literally carries information _____.

10. To <u>pre</u>dict a happening is to tell about it _____ it happens.

11. Something that is <u>im</u>measurable can _____ be measured.

12. The man's reasoning is <u>ir</u>rational; his thinking does _____ make sense.

13. Any material that can be <u>re</u>cycled can be used _____.

14. Anything that is <u>ir</u>revocable can _____ be called back.

15. A <u>per</u>ennial plant is one that grows _____ the year.

16. To <u>dis</u>honor a man's name is to take honor _____ his name.

17. When you <u>de</u>plane, you get _____ the plane.

18. To <u>mis</u>treat animals is to treat them _____.

A Directory of Drugs

Using the directory, answer the following:

1. Study the four classifications of drugs listed in heavy print. Give your own definition of what each of these words means to you.

2. How many drugs are derived from plants?

3. How many drugs are made synthetically? What does the word *synthetic* mean?

4. Many drugs are made synthetically. What is the implication of this for society?

5. How do you think some of these slang names originated? Check off the slang names of drugs that you know about or have heard mentioned.

6. Are there any known medical uses for hallucinogens?

7. Why do you think there is such a demand for depressants?

8. Under what classification of drugs do "pep pills" come?

9. What is another danger or risk involved in the prolonged use of drugs?

10. What are some of the ways to help people realize the dangers involved in taking drugs carelessly?

Drug	Slang Names	Description	Medical Use	Risks of Abuse
Hallucinogens				
Marijuana *Cannabis sativa*	Pot Grass Boo	Flowering, resinous top of female hemp plant	None	Altered perceptions, impaired judgment
Peyote *Lophophora williamsii*	Cactus	Dried cactus buttons containing mescaline. Chewed or brewed	Some experimental study	Visual hallucinations, anxiety, paranoia, possible pychosis
LSD *Lysergic acid diethylamide*	Acid Hawk The Chief	Synthetic chemical 400 times more powerful than mescaline	Some experimentation	Visual and auditory hallucinations, impaired judgment, possible psychosis

Stimulants

Cocaine *Erythroxylon coca*	Coke Corinne Happy dust Snow	Isolated alkaloid of coca leaf	Anesthesia of eye and throat	Loss of appetite, irritability, weight loss, insomnia
Benzedrine *Amphetamine sulphate*	A Bennies (Pep pills)	Synthetic central-nervous-system stimulant	Treatment of obesity, narcolepsy, encephalitis, fatigue, depression	Nausea, hypertension, irritability, confusion, delirium, aggressiveness
Dexedrine *Dextroampheta-mine sulphate*	A Dexies Copilots (Pep pills)	Same as above	Same as above	Same as above

Depressants

Nembutal *Pentobarbital sodium*	Yellow-jackets	Barbituric acid derivative	Sedation. Treatment of insomnia	Incoherency, depression, possible respiratory arrest, addiction with withdrawal symptoms including vomiting, tremors, convulsions
Seconal *Secobarbital sodium*	Red birds	Same as above	Same as above	Same as above
Amytal *Amobarbital sodium*	Blue heavens	Same as above	Same as above	Same as above
Miltown *Meprobamate*		Non-barbiturate sedatives	Same as above	Same as above
Librium *Chlordiazepoxide*		Tranquilizer	Treatment of anxiety, tension, alcoholism, neurosis	Blurring of vision, confusion, possible severe depression when combined with alcohol

Narcotics

Opium *Papaver somniferum (plant)*		Dried, coagulated milk of unripe opium-poppy pod	Treatment of pain, severe diarrhea	Loss of appetite, temporary impotency or sterility. Painful withdrawal symptoms
Morphine	M Miss Emma	10-1 reduction of crude opium	Treatment of severe pain	Same as above
Heroin	H Horse Junk Smack	Converted morphine	None	Same as above

71

Finding Words in the Dictionary

Does it seem to take forever to find a word in the dictionary? If it does, here's a tip that will speed up the task for you. First of all, remember the old nursery rhyme about the alphabet. It went something like this:

ABCDEFG
HIJKLMNOP
QRSTUVWXYZ

Think of your dictionary as having three parts: A-G, H-P, Q-Z. The idea is to open your dictionary as close as possible to the word you are looking for. With practice you should come within twenty pages of any word on the first attempt.

Practice the skill of opening your dictionary to the correct place.

1. Try opening your dictionary to some point within each of these pairs of letters:

S-C   P-U   B-Z   L-V   R-J

2. Try to open your dictionary within twenty pages of each of these words:

aspen   feat   knock   ermine   interior

wait   outlook   skirl   through   vestry

In the above exercise you were concerned with only the first letter of the words. Now you must think in terms of the other letters in order to locate a word alphabetically. You may need to use the first five or six letters, or even more, in order to find a word in your dictionary.

Number these sets of words 1, 2, 3, 4, in order of their appearance in the dictionary.

Use fourth letters	Use fifth letters	Use sixth letters
___ supraorbital	___ support	___ superficial
___ superb	___ supper	___ supersonic
___ supplant	___ suppress	___ superhighway
___ supinate	___ supple	___ superiority

Use seventh and eighth letters	Use tenth and eleventh letters
___ superphysical	___ supersensible
___ superpower	___ supersensual
___ superposed	___ supersensory
___ superphosphate	___ supersensitive

Guide words can also help you find words quickly. The guide word in the upper left-hand corner of a dictionary page is the *first* word defined on that page. The guide word in the upper right-hand corner is the *last* word defined. Therefore any word alphabetically between the guide words will be found on that page.

The following exercises will help you to use guide words. Each column is headed with guide words, as in a dictionary. Put a check beside the words that would appear on the page. For those that don't appear on the page, write B (Before) or A (After) to indicate the direction you would turn in your dictionary to find them.

enhance-enroll	gorgeous-gourde
1. endow ___	1. governess ___
2. enrage ___	2. gotten ___
3. enlist ___	3. gore ___
4. ensnare ___	4. gouge ___
5. ennui ___	5. Gorki ___

manicurist-mansion	Poland-politic
1. manner ___	1. polar ___
2. maple ___	2. polite ___
3. manhood ___	3. policy ___
4. manlike ___	4. polity ___
5. mantilla ___	5. poky ___

Parts Department: Roots

One way to develop a wide vocabulary is to learn the meanings of common roots that appear in words of our language. If you were to start with a single word and learn the meanings of the parts of that word, here's how it might work:

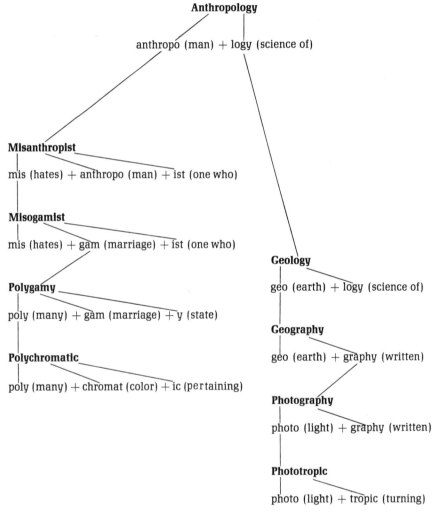

Anthropology

anthropo (man) + logy (science of)

Misanthropist

mis (hates) + anthropo (man) + ist (one who)

Misogamist

mis (hates) + gam (marriage) + ist (one who)

Polygamy

poly (many) + gam (marriage) + y (state)

Polychromatic

poly (many) + chromat (color) + ic (pertaining)

Geology

geo (earth) + logy (science of)

Geography

geo (earth) + graphy (written)

Photography

photo (light) + graphy (written)

Phototropic

photo (light) + tropic (turning)

Many of the above words appear to be very difficult when one first sees them. But, as you can see, they're really quite easy words to understand *if* you know the meaning of at least one part.

Below are listed several more roots (sometimes called combining forms), their meanings, and the language from which they come.

auto	self	*autos,*	Greek
bio	life	*bios,*	Greek
gon	angle	*gonia,*	Greek
meter	measure	*metrum,*	Latin
mit	send	*mittere,*	Latin
mono	one	*monos,*	Greek
phil	loving, fond of	*philos,*	Greek
phono	sound	*phone,*	Greek
psycho	mind, soul	*psyche,*	Greek
sopho	wisdom	*sophos,*	Greek

Let's try a simple word and see how it can lead us to the meaning of a more difficult word:

automobile

auto (self) + mobile (moving)

Now break **autobiography** into its parts and list the meanings.

_____ + _____ + _____

Write the meanings of these words:

1. psychology = _____ + _____

   meaning: _____

2. philanthropy = _____ + _____ + _____

   meaning: _____

3. monogamist = _____ + _____ + _____

   meaning: _____

4. phonograph = _____ + _____

   meaning: _____

Parts Department: Roots Review

Write the meanings of the roots and combining forms listed below.

1. polyphone = poly _____ + phone _____

2. autograph = auto _____ + graph _____

3. photograph = photo _____ + graph _____

4. chromometer = chromo _____ + meter _____

5. monochrome = mono _____ + chrome _____

6. biology = bio _____ + logy _____

7. photometer = photo _____ + meter _____

8. psychometer = psycho _____ + meter _____

9. biography = bio _____ + graphy _____

10. biogeography = bio _____ + geo _____ + graphy _____

11. phonometer = phono _____ + meter _____

12. polygon = poly _____ + gon _____

13. monograph = mono _____ + graph _____

14. philanthropist = phil _____ + anthrop _____
    + ist _____

15. philosophic = philo _____ + soph _____ + ic _____

16. sophist = soph _____ + ist _____

Old Riddles, Old Questions

Beyond the bright searchlights of science,
Out of sight of the windows of sense,
Old riddles still bid us defiance,
Old questions of Why and of Whence.

WILLIAM CECIL DAMPIER-WHETHAM

The Recent Development of Physical Science,
by William Cecil Dampier-Whetham, copyright
1904. By permission of John Murray (Publishers), Ltd.

Key Words

cacophony–harsh, clashing sound; expansive–wide, broad; acoustic–having to do with sound or hearing; refuge–shelter; contemporary–belonging in the same period of time

Urban Noise

Clifford R. Bragdon

Urban noise occurs around the clock. Garbage trucks announce the arrival of the day. In apartments, the sounds of the neighbor's children, pets, and television pierce the morning silence. On the way to work, general traffic din and the cacophony of building construction and street repair projects continuously assault the ears. The work environment is another auditory experience. Noise has been recognized for years as a problem in factories. Now general office design, with its expansive glass areas, open spaces, narrow partitions and hard acoustic surfaces, plus typewriters, telephones, air conditioners and business machines, may create noise exceeding industrial levels.

Home offers little refuge when the urban dweller returns in the evening. Our heating-ventilating systems, plumbing, and home appliances hiss, chug, hum, swish, and grind indoors. The walls of the house or apartment building only partially subdue the roar of automobile and air traffic from outside. All this makes us aware in mind and body that noise is an ever-present part of our contemporary urban life. (166 words)

True or False

Mark each statement either true (T) or false (F).

___ 1. Only recently has noise been recognized as a problem in factories.

___ 2. Home offers the only refuge that the urban dweller has from noise.

___ 3. Both our minds and our bodies are aware of noise.

Sound Sense: Diphthongs

Say these words: now, house. Did you notice that the <u>ow</u> and the <u>ou</u> stand for the same sound? Say these words: <u>noise</u>, <u>boys</u>. Did you notice that the <u>oi</u> and <u>oy</u> stand for the same sound? These pairs of vowels are called diphthongs. Each pair stands for a combined sound of two vowels. Now pronounce each word below. Circle the words in which ow and ou are sounded as they are in <u>now</u> and <u>house</u>. Underline the words in which <u>oi</u> and <u>oy</u> are sounded as they are in <u>noise</u> and <u>boys</u>.

1. cow	4. about	7. snow	10. blow	13. plow
2. you	5. destroy	8. loin	11. toy	14. flour
3. oil	6. through	9. join	12. enjoy	15. shout

Sound Sense: Vowel Review

Mark the vowels in the words below. Put ˘ over vowels that have a short sound; put ¯ over vowels that have a long sound; put / through vowels that are silent; underline diphthongs. For example: blŏckh<u>ou</u>se.

1. daydream	6. employ	11. glass
2. invade	7. concrete	12. crankcase
3. extreme	8. mind	13. transmit
4. hoist	9. foil	14. convoy
5. distaste	10. lifted	15. growl

Key Words
cleave-to split; *vaporize*-to change into mist or steam; *scythe*-a long, curved blade on a handle; *conceived*-imagined; *decade*-period of ten years

---

Laser Beams

Max Gunther

Beams that can slice buildings in half or cleave steel at a distance or vaporize aircraft or mow down men as a scythe mows grass. True or false? Reality or plan or merely a dream? The facts cannot be had.

The laser business is like that. Never before in history has a scientific invention gone from mental concept to working hardware to world-wide application in so short a time. The raw idea of a laser was conceived little more than a decade ago. The first working model was built three years later. Today lasers are used in surgery, welding, drilling, surveying, weaponry. They are common items of technological hardware, available by mail order like Bunsen burners or microscopes. They shouldn't really have arrived until the 21st Century. "It's like being shot into the future," says Alan Haley, regional sales manager at Perkin-Elmer. "I'm selling a product that didn't exist when I got out of college—wasn't conceived, wasn't even dreamed of. I'm selling it like ordinary hardware. I carry samples of it around. What would a career counselor have said ten or twenty years ago if I'd told him I wanted to sell ray guns for a living?" (198 words)

True or False

Mark each statement either true (T) or false (F).

___ 1. Laser beams may be used to slice buildings in half.

___ 2. The idea of a laser beam was conceived little more than a decade ago.

_____ 3. Lasers are difficult for the ordinary citizen to obtain.

_____ 4. The first working model of a laser was built two years after the idea was conceived.

_____ 5. The author implies that a vocational counselor ten years ago would have encouraged the student to sell ray guns for a living.

Parts Department: Suffixes

Notice what happens when you add suffixes to these words that end in _e_:

$$like + s = likes$$
$$like + ed = liked$$
$$like + ing = liking$$

Now complete the following statements.

1. When a suffix beginning with a _____ is added to a word ending in a final _e_, no change occurs in the spelling of the word.

2. When a suffix beginning with a _____ is added to a word ending in a final _e_, the _e_ is usually dropped.

Exception: When words ending in _ce_ and _ge_ are followed by a suffix beginning with _a_ or _o_, the final _e_ is _not_ dropped. For example:

$$courage + ous = courageous$$
$$notice + able = noticeable$$

Write the correct form of the new word.

3. tame + ed _____

4. change + ing _____

5. trace + able _____

6. dance + ed _____

7. lace + y _____

8. shine + s _____

9. dine + er _____

10. shame + ful _____

11. like + ly _____

12. care + less _____

Key Words

misnomer–a wrong name; botanical–having to do with plants; dormant–inactive; lure–to attract

Oh, Smart Man

Esther Henderson

The word "desert" is a misnomer when applied to the Southern Arizona region surrounding Tucson and Phoenix. More properly, this "desert" is a botanical wonder garden of exotic shapes, sizes, habits, colors, and varieties. Few areas in the world yield such plant diversity. It appears nowhere else within the continental United States.

As if this were not enough, periodically this area springs into fabulous bloom. Moisture alone is not the total explanation; the moisture must occur in the right quantities *and* at the right intervals and time. What a miracle it is that these seed casings, dormant for years under the broiling desert summer sun, yet sheltering the germ of life within, are never lured into bursting until all the conditions are favorable for the sprouting plant to complete its life cycle and form seeds for the next generation, however many years away that may be. Oh, smart Man, with your super-smart computers, compute the dates of the future flowerful years in the desert if you can! (167 words)

True or False

Mark each statement either true (T) or false (F).

___ 1. The word "desert" is a fitting name for the Southern Arizona region.

___ 2. Moisture is not the total explanation for the desert's blossoms.

___ 3. Seeds may lie dormant for years in the desert.

___ 4. The area described has only a few varieties of plants.

___ 5. The author implies that a computer has been developed that can accurately predict when the desert will bloom.

Parts Department: Suffixes

Look carefully at these words.

> stop + ed = stopped
> stoop + ed = stooped
> stomp + ed = stomped

Why was the p doubled in the first word and not in the next two words? Complete this statement.

1. When a suffix beginning with a vowel is added to a word that ends

   in a single _____ , preceded by a single _____ ,

   the final _____ may be doubled.

Watch it! The above statement applies *only* if the word is accented on its last syllable. For example:

> refer + ed = re ferred ´   refer + ence = ref´erence

Write the correct form of the words below. (Use your dictionary if you are not sure which syllable is accented.)

2. commit + ed _____

3. prefer + ing _____

4. prohibit + ing _____

5. open + er _____

6. submit + ed _____

7. permit + ed _____

8. gallop + ing _____

9. commit + ment _____

10. orbit + ed _____

11. gossip + y _____

12. design + er _____

13. appear + ance _____

14. allot + ment _____

15. prefer + ence _____

Pronunciation in the Dictionary

a	ā	ã	ä	e	ē	ėr	i	ī
hat	āge	cãre	fär	let	ēqual	tėrm	it	īce

o	ō	ô	oi	ou	u	u̇	ü	ch
hot	ōpen	ôrder	oil	out	cup	pu̇t	rüle	child

ng	th	ŦH	zh	ə represents **a** in about, **e** in taken,
long	thin	ŦHen	measure	**i** in pencil, **o** in lemon, **u** in circus

From *The World Book Dictionary* front matter. © 1969 Field Enterprises Educational Corporation.

Using the pronunciation key above, see if you can figure out what the following sentences say.

1. Grāt spen'·dərz är bad lü'·sərz. —Franklin

2. Līf iz mād up uv sobz, snif'·əlz, and smīlz, with snif'·əlz pri·dom'·ə·nāt·ing. —O. Henry

3. ə pik'·chər iz ə po'·əm with·out' werdz. —Horace

4. It mā mmāk ə dif'·ər·əns tü ôl i·ter'·nə·tē hweŦH'·ər wē dü rīt ôr rông tə·dā'. —James Freeman Clarke

5. ə·rij'·ə·nal'·ə·tē iz sim'·plē ə pãr uv fresh īz. —T. W. Higgins

The above sentences show how a dictionary uses phonetic respelling to help you pronounce unfamiliar words. A complete pronunciation key appears at the front of every dictionary. The key shows the symbols used for phonetic respelling in that dictionary. Many dictionaries also provide an abbreviated form of the key at the bottom of every right-hand page. It may look like this one:

PRONUNCIATION KEY: hat, āge, cãre, fär; let, ēqual, tėrm; it, īce; hot, ōpen, ôrder; oil, out; cup, pu̇t, rüle; child; long; thin, ŦHen; zh, measure; ə represents **a** in about, **e** in taken, **i** in pencil, **o** in lemon, **u** in circus.

From *The World Book Dictionary*. © 1969 Doubleday & Company, Inc.

Respell these words that are spelled phonetically.

1. thôt _____
2. f̄it _____
3. frēz _____
4. THēz _____
5. gėrl _____

6. ri plīd´ _____
7. rīt´ ing _____
8. pri zent´ _____
9. biz´ nis _____
10. ri serv´ _____

Spell these words phonetically.

11. way _____
12. fame _____
13. though _____
14. tie _____
15. thus _____

16. machine _____
17. alike _____
18. ocean _____
19. panic _____
20. throne _____

Gearing Up for Reading

You wouldn't think of taking a trip without first consulting a map. You'd first study the general route of your trip, and then you'd get down to considering the specific points of interest, places to stop, and possible side trips. In a similar manner, it is wise to "map out" something that you are going to read, in order to know where you're headed, the time it might require you to get there, and the pauses you might have to make along the way.

In the following selection, a title and sub-titles have been provided to map your route through the reading of the selection. Try turning the title and each sub-title into a question. For instance, "A Vision of the Year 2000" raises the question, "What exactly is the author taking a look at?" If you skim through the first paragraph, you quickly get a clue that the author is talking about a scientific and technological revolution. Now, look at each sub-title and turn it into a question; skim the paragraphs that fall under each sub-title. Do you see where you're going? Can you estimate the time required to read the selection carefully? As you read the selection, you should find that the details will fall neatly into place under the sub-titles that you have considered.

Key Words

technology—science of mechanical and industrial arts; solon—a member of the legislature; paradox—a contradictory fact; noxious—poisonous; artifact—anything made by human skill

---

A Vision of the Year 2000

Clare Boothe Luce

(1) *World-shaking Scientific and Technological Revolution.* It is time to take stock of the fact that we are living through the greatest revolution in the history of mankind. Its origins are rooted in the ancient past and in man's ancient yet ever modern thirst for knowledge and for power over his environment. This world-shaking revolution is the scientific and technological revolution of the twentieth century.

(2) The pace of science and of technology in the West had begun to quicken well before World War II. But it is their explosive rate of progress since then, especially in America, that now gives them their revolutionary character.

(3) For example, the New York World's Fair of 1939 chose as its theme "The World of Tomorrow." Its most spectacular exhibit was a scale model of a futuristic civilization in which mankind had intercontinental rocketry and atomic power. Guides who conducted open-mouthed visitors through the exhibit informed them that the scientists and technologists who had designed it were confident that rockets would come in one or two generations, though atomic power probably would be a matter of several centuries. Five years later, America had both.

(4) *Yesterday's Science Fiction a Reality Today.* During my first term in Congress (1942-44), if any Congressman had predicted that the United States would be spending billions within fewer than twenty years to land on the moon, the moonstruck solon might have landed back in private life after the next election. Unmanned spacecraft orbiting Mars; men walk-

ing in space, digging through the earth's crust on the ocean floor, perfecting "death rays" (lasers); submarines capable of firing intercontinental missiles from under water and cruising below polar floes; robot machines that not only could calculate production needs and consumer demands, but program their own work, make decisions, correct their own errors, digest and memorize millions of facts and figures and produce them in the twinkling of an eye—all such things, as we reached the mid-century mark, were still to be found only in science fiction, and in Buck Rogers and Superman comic strips. Today they, and much else that was incredible a few years ago, are realities.

(5) *Limitless Possibilities.* Our wildest speculations may seem merely timid predictions as we near the end of this century. Submarines that can fly? Vertical passenger-plane takeoffs? Planes carrying a thousand people? These are already on the drawing boards. A device to supply man with "gills," so he can breathe as easily in the ocean as he does on land? Sport submarines that can cruise for a weekend on the ocean's bottom? Engineering methods that will permit us to erect houses and hotels in the bosom of the sea? Accurate medical checkup and diagnoses made by computers? New eyes for old? New ears, hearts, kidneys, livers, bones for outworn or diseased ones? A life expectancy of a hundred years? All these things are quite possible in the lifetime of millions of Americans. The great breakthrough—the discovery of how to dissolve the field of gravity, so man can hover above the earth in giant aircraft or sky houses and observatories? A way to control volcanoes, so they will create new islands for our constantly expanding population to inhabit? Maybe not for centuries— but maybe before our children become grandparents.

(6) Only one thing can we predict with any certainty: if the revolution is *not* stopped, life in America in the year 2000 will be as different from life here today as life today differs from life in 1800. And over fifty percent of our population will be living in the super-revolutionary year 2000!

(7) *Need to Control Technological Revolution.* How should a free and democratic people set about controlling this revolu-

tion? Already many American leaders are arguing the urgent need for control. The problem—and paradox—of crushing poverty in an age of limitless plenty challenges the dullest political minds.

(8) We are beginning to realize that unemployment among unskilled and semi-skilled workers must steadily increase as automation phases out their jobs. We know it is daily more necessary to plan jobs now for millions of idle hands who will otherwise be employed by the Devil. We suspect that if we are to keep consumer dollars flowing into industry, we may have to guarantee an annual income for all our adults and may even have to pay our young people to go to college, so they won't turn to crime, for want of job opportunities. We are beginning to realize that we will have to shorten the work week by days, not hours, if we are to maintain even nominal full employment.

(9) But as a nation we are still far from aware of how tragically we have failed to control some of the physical side effects of the revolution.

(10) *Problems Created.* We have let our superb industrial plants dump their refuse into all our river systems and inland-ocean lakes, turning even the mighty Hudson and Mississippi into poisonous sewers and our Great Lakes into cesspools. We have let our industrial machines and automobiles fill the skies over our cities with noxious gases and industrial dirt of every kind. In a technological age that could easily provide disposal plants and filter systems for air and water pollutants, we are permitting the revolution to filter its noisome wastes through our stomachs and lungs.

(11) We have refused to make government, industry or ourselves responsible for disposing decently of the corpses of our worn-out mechanical household slaves—refrigerators, television sets and other equipment destined for the junkyard. The ugly, rusty, twisted bodies of our most idolized machine, the automobile, have piled up along our highways. We have increased the scandal of the automobile graveyard with the scandal of roadside litter. Every day, tons of bottles, cans, boxes, papers, food remnants, cigarette butts and other rub-

bish are thrown out of car windows onto the roadside.

(12) *Adequate Program Needed.* It has been estimated that an adequate program to provide clean air, clean water and clean highways for citizens of the future will cost 50 billion dollars. But if we do not very soon undertake this program, by the year 2000, Americans will be living in an Augean stable. At this point, the country is likely to become a nation of emigrants. The tremendous population shift to the West in the past ten years is partially due to the desires of millions to escape the disgusting side effects of the revolution. But when, even in the West, people no longer can see the stars at night for the smog, they will begin to leave America itself....

(13) *Two Choices.* Looking in the New Year's crystal ball, I see two pictures forming for the year 2000. In one, thousands of Americans are leaving for lands — any land, however "backward" — where there are green hills and blue skies and sweet waters. Australia, New Zealand, Africa, Latin America. Islands where the winds broom white clouds and where birds sing in occasional parks and forests. Such lands are beckoning Americans, in full flight from the vast slum made of their own country.

(14) In the second picture, I see a fair land, full of shining buildings and extraordinary new machines and artifacts, whose uses I am unable to imagine — any more than I could have imagined what a radio or television was for, had I seen their forms in a crystal ball in my youth. I also see sights I once was familiar with: old men fishing and young people swimming in the wide, clean rivers that flow through cities...small children playing in the shade of great trees along flower-bordered highways...lovers walking through city parks under a clear midnight moon, unafraid of muggers.

(15) *Our Ultimate Goal.* But I also see a new sight: magnificent universities with garden campuses, where the youth of our land is being trained to direct the revolution for the betterment of mankind. And I seem to hear a professor explaining that, along about 1966, the American people began to fight the war against poverty. Not against material poverty only, but against poverty of spirit. "America," this professor is say-

ing, "awoke somewhat late to the fact that it is not enough for a great nation of free men to be strong and rich in material things. It must be rich in spirit, rich in imagination, rich in courage—and it must desire to create a beautiful as well as a prosperous country. So the American people began to control the scientific and technological revolution. This revolution is still presenting us with many problems; but thanks to the actions begun thirty years ago, we of the twenty-first century know we can solve them." (1432 words)

Time:_____

Talk It Over

Discuss these questions. Review them, if you want, by referring to the paragraph number in parentheses.

1. What is behind man's progress in technology? (1)
2. What are some of the "impossible feats" of yesteryear that are realities today? (4)
3. What are some of the predictions for the end of this century? (5)
4. What employment problems are created by automation? (8)
5. What may be some of the tragic aftermaths of the "off-balance" between our natural resources and technology? (9-10)
6. What is meant by "Americans will be living in an Augean stable"? (12)
7. What are the two pictures the author sees in the New Year's crystal ball? (13-14)
8. In the first picture, where are some of the places Americans may go? (13)
9. In the second picture, we are looking at an "ideal" condition. What might make this possible? (14)
10. What is the message that Clare Boothe Luce is trying to tell us? (15)

Analogies

Historical and Geographical Analogies. In each of the following items, underline the term that is related to the third term in the same way as the second term is related to the first.

1. United Nations is to New York as UNESCO is to (London) (Paris) (Stockholm) (Moscow).

2. Sunflower State is to Kansas as Bluegrass State is to (Ohio) (Kentucky) (Virginia) (Tennessee).

3. George Washington is to John Adams as Lyndon B. Johnson is to (Harry Truman) (Dwight Eisenhower) (Hubert Humphrey) (Robert F. Kennedy).

4. Little Giant is to Stephen A. Douglas as Little Corporal is to (Lord Nelson) (Napoleon Bonaparte) (Cornwallis) (Lord Halifax).

5. Alaska is to Russia as Louisiana Purchase is to (Spain) (England) (France) (Mexico).

6. New Deal is to Franklin D. Roosevelt as New Frontier is to (Dwight Eisenhower) (John F. Kennedy) (Herbert Hoover) (Lyndon B. Johnson).

7. Disneyland is to California as Yellowstone National Park is to (North Dakota) (Utah) (Wyoming) (Nebraska).

8. John Glenn is to Friendship 7 as Alan B. Shepard is to (Discoverer 7) (Freedom 7) (Explorer 7) (Ranger 7).

9. Mt. Fuji is to Japan as Mt. Vesuvius is to (Spain) (Italy) (Portugal) (Greece).

10. Mississippi River is to Gulf of Mexico as Amazon River is to (Caribbean Sea) (Atlantic Ocean) (Pacific Ocean) (Mediterranean Sea).

11. The Alps are to Switzerland as the Catskills are to (Colorado) (Vermont) (New York) (Idaho).

12. The White House is to Washington, D.C., as (Windsor Castle) (the Bastille) (Buckingham Palace) (Hampton Court) is to London.

13. The Eiffel Tower is to Paris as the Leaning Tower is to (Rome) (Venice) (Pisa) (Verona).

14. The Nile is to Egypt as the Thames is to (France) (Belgium) (Scotland) (England).

Growth Jobs Requiring Training

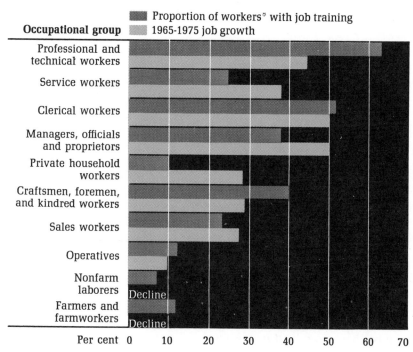

Occupational group

■ Proportion of workers* with job training
▨ 1965-1975 job growth

Professional and technical workers

Service workers

Clerical workers

Managers, officials and proprietors

Private household workers

Craftsmen, foremen, and kindred workers

Sales workers

Operatives

Nonfarm laborers — Decline

Farmers and farmworkers — Decline

Per cent 0   10   20   30   40   50   60   70

*Excluding college graduates, 1963

From *The World Book Year Book.* © 1968 Field Enterprises Educational Corporation.

Use the graph to answer and discuss these questions:

1. What occupational group has the greatest percentage of job training? (Why do you think this particular group has need of continuous job training?)

2. What group shows a relatively equal growth in both job training and job growth?

3. What does the graph tell us about the occupational group of managers, officials, and proprietors?

4. What does the graph tell us about craftsmen, foremen, and kindred workers?

Would You Believe?

If the word *migrant* [< Latin, *migrare,* move + *ant,* one who] means one who moves from one place to another, then what is

an *emigrant?* _____

_____

an *immigrant?* _____

_____

a *migratory* worker? _____

The word *revolve* means to move in a circle or around a central point [< Latin, *revolvere* < *re-,* back, again + *volvere,* to roll]. What is the meaning of the italicized words in these sentences?

He was a soldier in the *revolution.* _____

_____

I have been *involved* in my work. _____

_____

They *evolved* a plan for making money. _____

_____

Joe watched the *convolutions* of the snake. _____

The word *democracy* means a government that is run by the people who live under it [< Greek, *demokratia* < *demos,* people + *kratos,* rule, power]. What, then, is a

demographer? _____

demophile? _____

Reading the Newspaper

Efficiency should be one of your goals in reading. One type of reading you do frequently is reading a newspaper. The table of contents, usually printed on the first page, can help you use the paper more efficiently. The following exercise is designed to show you some of the things you can find quickly by using a table of contents. Note that the section of the newspaper is referred to by letter; the page, by number.

In the Paper Today

Business and Finance B5-6
Classified Advertising C11-14
Comics B10-12
Editorials C16
Entertainment B4
Local News A10
Medical Column A8

Politics by Perry A6
Social Activities B1-3
Sports C1-6
Television and Radio C8
Vital Statistics C10
Weather C9

Study the above table of contents. Write down the section and page number or numbers where you would find these items.

1. Previews of TV movies _____

2. A 1965 Chevrolet for sale _____

3. Medical advice _____

4. Tom Carroll's column "Behind the Sports Scene" _____

5. What's playing this week at the drive-in _____

6. Stock exchange news _____

7. Whether it's going to rain tomorrow _____

8. Deborah Frothingham's engagement to Milton Manypenny ____

9. Political commentary _____

10. The story of last night's apartment-building fire _____

Parts Department: Suffixes

Certain suffixes mean *who* or *what*: -ance, -ment, -ion, -er, -or, -ant. Each of these suffixes, when added to a word, changes the meaning to "one who," "that which," or "condition or state of." In other words, these suffixes are really endings that *name* somebody or something.

In the spaces below, add suffixes to the words given, to form new words. (Some words may take more than one suffix.)

rob _____ _____

perform _____ _____

assign _____ _____

audit _____ _____

connect _____ _____

act _____ _____

collect _____ _____

clear _____ _____

agree _____ _____

allow _____ _____

protect _____ _____

improve _____ _____

Can you complete this paragraph by adding words from the list above?

As a _____ in the circus, he had the _____

of providing _____ for the animals. He had made an

_____ with his boss that he would always work toward

the _____ of the acts in the show.

You Are What You Value

The fact that man knows right from wrong
proves his intellectual superiority to the other
creatures; but the fact that he can do wrong
proves his moral inferiority to any creature
that cannot.

MARK TWAIN

Key Words

<u>vent</u>–to relieve or unburden; <u>*self-esteem*</u>–thinking well of oneself

---

Right or Wrong?

Ann Landers

Parents must accept the fact that there will be moments when their children will hate them. This is normal and it is natural. But how a child handles hate may determine whether he will go to Harvard or to San Quentin. A child should be taught to vent his anger in socially acceptable ways — ways that will not injure others, damage property, or hurt his own self-esteem. Rules should be established and limits set — in writing, if necessary. I cannot emphasize too strongly the importance of setting limits. The child who knows exactly how far he can go is relieved of a heavy burden.

In our family the rules were simple: get as mad as you like, but there must be no hitting, no yelling swear words so loud that the neighbors will hear, and no breaking anything you aren't prepared to pay for. (144 words)

True or False

Mark each statement either true (T) or false (F).

___ 1. Children's hate is abnormal and unnatural.

___ 2. If rules are established, they're sure to be broken.

___ 3. Children are relieved when they know their limits.

___ 4. A child can be taught to express his anger properly.

___ 5. The author implies that it's all right to use swear words as long as the neighbors don't hear you.

Key Words

compassion-sympathy; *status*-state or condition

Beyond Self

Everyone has a chance to live and to love beyond himself, but how many of us really do? For far too many people, the area of concern is a small one: *my* job, *my* family, *my* possessions, *my* friends. But a person is not really fulfilled until he has learned to set aside concern for self and to extend concern and compassion for the other fellow. It is not true that the most secure person is the one who has satisfied his own needs and no one else's. But it *is* true that some of the most secure people are those who have given their time, their talents, and their friendship to others, without expecting anything in return. We may never really know what we've accomplished when we've helped another human being, but the simple act of giving is a reward in itself. If man belongs to man, then barriers of race, religion, and financial status must never prevent us from offering a helping hand to the other fellow. Just the act of offering—of saying, in a sense, that we care—may make the life of the giver a richer one. (192 words)

True or False

Mark each statement either true (T) or false (F).

___ 1. When you give, you should get something in return.

___ 2. People who have everything are not always secure.

___ 3. We always know what we've accomplished when we've helped another person.

___ 4. The author implies that the really fulfilled person is the one who asks for and receives help from another person.

Key Words

flagrant–outrageous; *hallmark*–a symbol of high quality

Why Fear?

Ann Landers

Juvenile delinquency is at an all-time high, and the authorities point out that a staggering number of delinquents come from the so-called "better" homes. Never in the history of our country has there been such flagrant disregard for law and order among 13- to 18-year-olds. The reasons cited? Teen-agers have no respect for authority. They fear no one. They grew up sassing their parents, talking back to their teachers, and finally they ran afoul of the law.

Am I suggesting that fear is a good thing? Yes, I am. Fear under certain circumstances is healthy and desirable. I am not recommending that children be terrified of their parents; there must be free and open expression on both sides, but the *manner* of expression should bear the hallmark of respect. (129 words)

True or False

Mark each statement either true (T) or false (F).

___ 1. Most juvenile delinquents come from poor homes.

___ 2. Teen-agers do not respect authority because they fear all authorities.

___ 3. Fear may be both healthy and desirable.

___ 4. Children should be taught to fear their parents.

___ 5. The author implies that some fear of authority can be desirable.

Sound Sense: R After a Vowel

Say these words: *word, far, stir, here, turn.* Did you notice that the r after the vowel influences the sound that the vowel stands for? Usually, when a vowel comes before r, that vowel stands for neither its long nor its short sound. Notice the sound for which the italicized e stands in these words:

here   there   were

Since the r is such a rule-breaker, you really can't depend on how these words sound in order to spell them correctly. A *visual* memory of the word is therefore necessary.

Can you fit the correctly spelled word into each of these sentences?

1. He drove a _____ to pull the plow.
   (tractor, tracter)

2. The animal's _____ was thick and warm.
   (fir, fer, fur)

3. She was a _____ in her father's store.
   (clurk, clirk, clerk)

Correctly spell the incomplete words below by writing *ar, er, or, ir,* or *ur* in the blanks.

4. On New Year's Day we throw out our old calend____s.

5. The diver came to the s____face of the lake.

6. The politician always sk____ts the issues.

7. We are planning a s____prise party for Dad.

8. What is the p____pose of this meeting?

9. The woods are full of maidenhair f____ns.

10. Jim is a contract____ for the government.

Reading a Table of Contents

To make the most effective use of a book, it is important that you develop your skill in reading its table of contents. This often neglected part of a book can, if used properly, save you a great deal of time in finding information you need.

The following table of contents is from Doris Gilbert's book, *Breaking the Reading Barrier*. Study the table of contents and then do the exercise that follows it.

Contents

Contents (cont'd)

Write the page number on which you would find the following:

1. a general statement about the purpose of this book _____

2. information for the instructor on administering tests printed in this book _____

3. a statement by the author about what the book will do for the reader _____

4. a plan for your reading practice time _____

5. a list of words to study for vocabulary improvement _____

6. a discussion of interpreting phrases rapidly _____

7. a test to measure your vocabulary _____

8. information on books for practicing reading skills _____

9. the steps on how to read more rapidly _____

10. procedures on how to write a report on a biography you've read _____

11. information on the importance of sentence reading _____

12. a discussion on main ideas of paragraphs _____

Analogies

Choose the term that best completes these analogies. Use your dictionary, or other reference, if necessary.

1. bevy : quails—(dogs : pack) (cars : fleet) (books : volume) (school : fish)

2. potato : Idaho—(Hawaii : sugar) (corn : Iowa) (Pittsburgh : coal) (salmon : Alaska)

3. musty : fragrant—monopoly : (mystery) (exclusiveness) (uniform) (competition)

4. cease : pause—(benefit : good) (nonsense : reason) (gentle : rough) (gradual : sudden)

5. "The world must be made safe for democracy" : Woodrow Wilson—"Give me liberty or give me death" : (Henry Clay) (Daniel Webster) (Patrick Henry) (John Calhoun)

6. 1 : 3—20 : (50) (40) (70) (60)

7. loose : secure—lose : (hide) (recover) (prove) (misplace)

8. Brooklyn Bridge : New York—Golden Gate Bridge : (Oregon) (Washington) (California) (Alaska)

9. dog : canine—(cat : pet) (cow : bovine) (horse : ride) (bird : aviary)

10. United Nations is to 1945 as League of Nations is to (1920) (1950) (1930) (1940)

Performing Specific Tasks

Following directions for a specific task requires a special reading skill. The following paragraphs give you directions for preparing a surface and painting it. Read them carefully, then answer the questions following, to test your ability to understand some of the important steps in the procedure.

General Surface Preparation

Remove all dirt, grease, or loose and scaling paint. Roughen all slick or glossy surfaces with sandpaper. Remove any mildew by washing with a solution of one pint of a household sodium hypochlorite bleach to a gallon of water. Rinse off this solution with clean water.

General Application

Latex house paint should not be applied when the outside temperature is less than 50° F. Such low temperature during the drying period will prevent proper curing of the paint film. Application can be done with either brush, roller, or spray equipment. To obtain the best results, apply with a nylon brush or dynel-type roller. Latex house paint is so easy to apply and spreads so freely that it is possible to cover too great an area with too little paint. It should be applied generously in a full, even coat. Excessive brushing should be avoided. Do not exceed more than 450 square feet per gallon. Latex house paint will dry tack-free in about 30 minutes; a second coat should not be applied until the first coat is thoroughly hard and cured.

1. What is scaling paint? _____

_____

2. What will a sodium hypochlorite bleach solution do to mildew?

_____

3. Why is clean water used in the procedure? _____

_____

4. When should this latex house paint *not* be applied? _____

_____

5. What two ways are recommended for application? _____

_____

Sound Sense: The Sounds of S

Say these words and notice the different sound for which the s stands in each: was, same, sugar, measure. Place each of the following words in the correct row according to its s sound.

sure	treasure	makes	has
lose	pension	surf	does
suit	leisure	fusion	comprehension
present	purse	busy	tension

1. s as in *same* (s) _____

2. s as in *sugar* (sh) _____

3. s as in *was* (z) _____

4. s as in *measure* (zh) _____

Sound Sense: The Sounds of C

The letter c can stand for two sounds—a soft sound and a hard sound. When c is followed by e, i, or y, it has a soft sound, as in cent, city, and icy. When c is followed by a, o, or u, it has a hard sound, as in car, cot, and cut. Identify the sound of c in the words below. Put H in the blank if the c has a hard sound; put S if it has a soft sound.

___ 1. century   ___ 6. success   ___11. center

___ 2. cyanide   ___ 7. America   ___12. notice

___ 3. carry   ___ 8. coincide   ___13. consonant

___ 4. vacate   ___ 9. citation   ___14. office

___ 5. cigar   ___10. voice   ___15. custom

Words You Need

Read each sentence and choose the meaning of the word in italics. Write the letter of your answer on the line. Use your dictionary if necessary.

Check the correct definition:

___ 1. His attitude that "you can't believe anyone nowadays" had a quality of *cynicism* in it.

Cynicism means: a) unhappiness; b) distrust; c) regret.

___ 2. "What's that plumber's name?" was my mother's *implication* that I couldn't fix the leak.

Implication means: a) indirect suggestion; b) evidence; c) nasty attitude.

___ 3. We knew that *extortioners* were at work when we heard that the grocer's store was wrecked because he would not pay a gambling debt.

Extortioners means: a) those who use illegal means to get something from a person; b) those who beat up people; c) those who take bets from gamblers.

___ 4. Seeing that he could do nothing to aid the injured boy gave him a feeling of *impotence*.

Impotence means: a) anger; b) power; c) helplessness.

___ 5. For a professional athlete to be defeated by an amateur is to be defeated *ignominiously*.

Ignominiously means: a) shamefully; b) openly; c) badly.

___ 6. The *indulgent* mother gave her son everything he wanted.

Indulgent means: a) loving; b) permissive; c) kind.

___ 7. Mr. Grimes was *absolved* from all blame when the missing file was found on the president's desk.

Absolved means: a) absorbed; b) cleared; c) accused.

___ 8. *Archaic* statues were dug up from the buried ruins of old Greek cities.

Archaic means: a) broken; b) rusted; c) ancient.

___ 9. There are many words in the *lexicon* of youth that are unknown to their parents.

Lexicon means: a) vocabulary; b) experience; c) slang.

The Thin Grey Line

Marya Mannes

(1) "Aw, they all do it," growled the cabdriver. He was talking about cops who took payoffs for winking at double parking, but his cynicism could as well have been directed at any of a dozen other instances of corruption, big-time and small-time. Moreover, the disgust in his voice was overlaid by an unspoken "So what?": the implication that since this was the way things were, there was nothing anybody could do.

(2) Like millions of his fellow Americans, the cabdriver was probably a decent human being who had never stolen anything, broken any law or willfully injured another; somewhere, a knowledge of what was probably right had kept him from committing what was clearly wrong. But that knowledge had not kept a thin grey line that separates the two conditions from being daily greyer and thinner—to the point that it was hardly noticeable.

(3) On one side of this line are They: the bribers, the cheaters, the chiselers, the swindlers, the extortioners. On the other side are We—both partners and victims. They and We are now so perilously close that the only mark distinguishing us is that They get caught and We don't.

(4) The same citizen who voices his outrage at police corruption will slip the traffic cop on his block a handsome Christmas present in the belief that his car, nestled under a "No Parking" sign, will not be ticketed. The son of that nice woman next door has a habit of stealing cash from her purse because his allowance is smaller than his buddies'. Your son's friend admitted cheating at exams because "everybody does it."

(5) Bit by bit, the resistance to and immunity against wrong that a healthy social body builds up by law and ethics and the dictation of conscience have broken down. And instead of the fighting indignation of a people outraged by those who prey on them, we have the admission of impotence: "They all do it."

(6) Now, failure to uphold the law is no less corrupt than violation of the law. And the continuing shame of this country now is the growing number of Americans who fail to uphold and assist enforcement of the law, simply—and ignominiously—out of fear. Fear of "involvement," fear of reprisal, fear of "trouble." A man is beaten by hoodlums in plain daylight and in view of bystanders. These people not only fail to help the victim, but, like the hoodlums, flee before the police can question them. A city official knows of a colleague's bribe but does not report it. A pedestrian watches a car hit a woman but leaves the scene, to avoid giving testimony. It happens every day. And if the police get cynical at this irresponsibility, they are hardly to blame. Morale is a matter of giving support and having faith in one another; where both are lacking, "law" has become a worthless word.

(7) How did we get this way? What started this blurring of what was once a thick black line between the lawful and the lawless? What makes a "regular guy," a decent fellow, accept a bribe? What makes a nice kid from a middle-class family take money for doing something he must know is not only illegal but wrong?

(8) When you look into the background of an erring "kid" you will often find a comfortable home and a mother who will tell you, with tears in her eyes, that she "gave him everything." She probably did, to his everlasting damage. Fearing her son's disapproval, the indulgent mother denies him nothing except responsibility. Instead of growing up, he grows to believe that the world owes him everything.

(9) The nice kid's father crosses the thin grey line himself in a dozen ways, day in and day out. He pads his expenses on his income-tax returns as a matter of course. As a landlord, he pays the local inspectors of the city housing authority to

overlook violations in the houses he rents. When his son flunked his driving test, he gave him ten dollars to slip to the inspector on his second test. "They all do it," he said.

(10) The nice kid is brought up with boys and girls who have no heroes except people not much older than themselves who have made the Big Time, usually in show business or in sports. Publicity and money are the halos of their stars, who range from pop singers who can't sing to ballplayers who can't read; from teen-age starlets who can't act to television performers who can't think. They may be excited by the exploits of spacemen, but the work's too tough and dangerous.

(11) The nice kids have no heroes because they don't believe in heroes. Heroes are suckers and squares. To be a hero you have to stand out, to excel, to take risks, and above all, not only choose between right and wrong, but defend the right and fight the wrong. This means responsibility—and who needs it?

(12) Today, no one has to take any responsibility. The psychiatrists, the sociologists, the novelists, the playwrights have gone a long way to help promote irresponsibility. Nobody really is to blame for what he does. It's Society. It's Environment. It's a Broken Home. It's an Underprivileged Area. But it's hardly ever You.

(13) Now we find a truckload of excuses to absolve the individual from responsibility for his actions. A fellow commits a crime because he's basically insecure, because he hated his stepmother at nine, or because his sister needs an operation. A policeman loots a store because his salary is too low. A city official accepts a payoff because it's offered to him. Members of minority groups, racial or otherwise, commit crimes because they can't get a job, or are unacceptable to the people living around them. The words "right" and "wrong" are foreign to these people.

(14) But honesty is the best policy. Says who? Anyone willing to get laughed at. But the laugh is no laughing matter. It concerns the health and future of a nation. It involves the two-dollar illegal bettor as well as the corporation price-fixer, the college-examination cheater and the payroll-padding Congress-

man, the expense-account chiseler, the seller of pornography and his schoolboy reader, the bribed judge and the stealing delinquent. All these people may represent a minority. But when, as it appears now, the majority excuse themselves from responsibility by accepting corruption as natural to society ("They all do it"), this society is bordering on total confusion. If the line between right and wrong is finally erased, there is no defense against the power of evil.

(15) Before this happens—and it is by no means far away—it might be well for the schools of the nation to substitute for the much-argued issue of prayer a daily lesson in ethics, law, and responsibility to society that would strengthen the conscience as exercise strengthens muscles. And it would be even better if parents were forced to attend it. For corruption is not something you read about in the papers and leave to courts. We are all involved. (1172 words)

Time:_____

True or False

Mark each statement either true (T) or false (F).

___ 1. The thin grey line represents the diminishing line that separates right from wrong.

___ 2. When the cabdriver said, "They all do it," he was talking about students cheating at exams.

___ 3. A citizen who is outraged at police corruption would never be guilty of slipping money to "take care of" a traffic ticket.

___ 4. The police are the only public officials who cannot accept bribes.

___ 5. Youngsters who become involved in wrongdoings are invariably from underprivileged minority groups.

___ 6. One factor which encourages a person to commit wrongdoings is that society makes excuses for his behavior.

___ 7. When a nice youngster from a middle-class family takes money for something, he doesn't really realize that he's committing a crime.

Parts Department: Suffixes That Describe

-able	-al	-ant	-ary	-ed	-en	-ent	-ful
-ible	-ic	-ish	-less	-ous	-some	-y	

Each of these suffixes when added to a noun or verb changes the word to a describer, or an adjective. In other words, these suffixes are *adjective* endings. In the sentences below, complete each word with a suffix to complete the meaning of the sentence. Be careful of your spelling.

1. I am thank_____ that you have helped me.

2. That is not a suit_____ coat for this weather.

3. Sunday was a cold, snow_____ day.

4. This has been a joy_____ occasion for all of us.

5. John's work adds an artist_____ touch to our paper.

6. The face of a beard_____ man appeared at the window.

7. Each animal was in a comfort_____ enclosure in the zoo.

8. Use a wood_____ spoon for stirring the batter.

9. The mountains were an awe_____ sight for the visitors.

10. The king made a triumph_____ entry into the city.

11. He used an absorb_____ cloth to remove the water.

12. For years they owned a worth_____ piece of land.

13. He had served as a mission_____ doctor in Africa.

14. His actions are often child_____.

15. Copper is an impress_____ metal.

Would You Believe?

Many common words that we use have interesting histories, but because they are common, we seldom think of their origins. The word *neighbor* is an example that you have used frequently, but what does it mean?

[Old English *neahgebur* < nēah, nigh + gebūr, dweller]

Parts Department: Suffix Review

Complete the sentences by adding suffixes to the words on the lines. Make any necessary changes in spelling.

1. Ted purchased a port____ color television set.

2. You must learn to be more independ____ if you wish to live alone.

3. Her gold____ hair shone in the sunlight.

4. My mother was very critic____ of my new outfit.

5. Her appearance is very girl____ .

6. Don't worry; your fears are ground____ .

7. The play____ kitten knocked over a vase of flowers.

8. You certainly have some revolution____ ideas.

9. The children were frightened by the spook____ sound.

10. That field trip we took was very hazard____ .

11. The apples were very taste____ .

12. You are becoming very care____ with your spelling.

13. Soldiers in battle are very courage____ .

14. My collapse____ bike is easy to put in the car.

15. It's a pleasure to be with Joy; she's such a cheer____ person.

16. Those seat belts are adjust____ .

17. Her fancy gestures are very exaggerate____ .

18. She is always dressed in style____ clothes.

Would You Believe?

A figure of speech is a word or expression whose meaning is different from what its words actually say. For example, "He is a giant among men" obviously doesn't refer to his physical measurements but to some outstanding thing he may have done. These expressions may remain in the language long after their original meaning has been forgotten. For instance, "a chip off the old block" came from the stonecutter's trade. It meant that a piece off the original block had the same qualities as the original. The expression now means that a person may be very much like a parent in appearance or in personality.

Below are some common figures of speech. Match them to their original meanings.

    a) He's *as mad as a hatter.*

    b) I'd say that he's a man who really *knows the ropes.*

    c) What you've said really *goes against the grain.*

    d) Don't try to *soft-soap* me with your flattery!

    e) He's a *ham* if I ever saw one.

    f) I really passed the *acid test* to get my job.

___ 1. In early sailing days, each sailor had to know all about ropes and knots.

___ 2. A semiliquid variety of a cleansing agent; hence, to grease someone over with smooth words.

___ 3. At one time, poor actors used the fat from the leg of the hog to remove their makeup.

___ 4. Cutting across the grain of wood causes splinters or torn bits of wood.

___ 5. At one time, nitric acid was used to determine whether or not gold was contained in a substance.

___ 6. Men who made felt hats for people used mercury to work the felt properly. The mercury had a poisonous effect, which caused the hatter to twitch. He wasn't mad, but his twitching caused people to think that he was.

Definitions in the Dictionary

One of the major functions of your dictionary is to define words. It pays you to examine definitions carefully. Look at this dictionary entry of the word *cord* and answer the following questions.

cord (kôrd), *n.* **1.** a thick string; very thin rope. **2.** anything resembling a cord. **3.** a small, flexible, insulated cable with fittings, used to connect an electrical appliance, as an iron or a lamp, to a socket. **4.** *Anatomy.* a structure in an animal body that is somewhat like a cord, as a nerve or tendon. **5. a.** a ridge or ridged pattern on the surface of cloth. **b.** a cloth with such ridges on it, especially corduroy. **6.** any influence that binds, draws, or restrains as by cords: *The very sight of the island had relaxed the cords of discipline* (Robert Louis Stevenson). **7. a.** a measure of cut wood; 128 cubic feet. A pile of wood 4 feet wide, 4 feet high, and 8 feet long is a cord. **b.** the amount of wood in a pile of these dimensions: *$20 a cord for oak.* **8.** a hangman's rope: *the stake and the cord* (John Morley).
cords, trousers made of corduroy: *... our sprightly gentleman in the scarlet jacket and white cords* (Theodore Hook).
—*v.t.* **1.** to fasten or tie with a cord or cords: *He packed, locked, and corded his trunk.* **2.** to provide with a cord or cords: *The window sashes need to be corded.* **3.** to pile (wood) in cords: *They [trees] should be cut and corded before spring* (Emerson).
[< Old French *corde* < Latin *chorda* < Greek *chordē* gut. Compare CHORD².] —**cord'er,** *n.*

From *The World Book Dictionary.* © 1969 Doubleday & Company, Inc.

1. How many different definitions are there for the word *cord*?

_____

2. Why are the first eight definitions grouped together? _____

_____

3. What does the abbreviation v.t. stand for? _____

_____

4. Why does the word *cords* appear within this entry? _____

_____

5. Why is the definition "a thick string; very thin rope" given first?

_____

Even though the most common definition is given first in most dictionaries, you must develop the habit of looking beyond this definition when you look up an unfamiliar word. Writers use words in unusual ways to create special effect or emphasis.

Match the correct definition of the word *cord* to the way it is used in these sentences. Write the number of the verb or noun definition from the dictionary on the line before the sentence.

_____ 1. The *cord* connecting the bicep muscle to the lower arm was damaged in the accident.

_____ 2. The *cords* of matrimony held Eric firmly in his place.

_____ 3. The Post Office insisted the package be tied with heavier *cord*.

_____ 4. It was a hard summer's job to *cord* the oak logs against the side of the toolshed.

_____ 5. Roy purchased his usual *cord* of oak for the winter.

_____ 6. The judge ordered the *cord* readied for the horse thief.

_____ 7. *Cord* curtains were a bright addition to Sharon's kitchen.

_____ 8. It used to be the practice to wear your *cords* until they were so dirty they could stand by themselves in a corner.

_____ 9. After plugging in the *cord*, Marlene waited for the iron to heat.

_____10. Before departing, Father checked again to see if the load had been properly *corded* down.

Skills Review

Vowels. Mark the vowels in the words below. Place ˘ over vowels that have a short sound; place ˉ over vowels that have a long sound; put /

through vowels that are silent; underline the diphthongs. For example: bēcāme̸.

1. biceps	6. subsoil	11. struck
2. jowl	7. accept	12. psyche
3. mistake	8. create	13. grieve
4. coil	9. paintbox	14. coincide
5. hypnosis	10. employee	15. cyclone

Plurals. Write the plural form for each of these words.

1. business _____   6. phrase _____

2. attorney _____   7. muffin _____

3. brush _____   8. Friday _____

4. dictionary _____   9. century _____

5. sheriff _____   10. ax _____

Roots. Underline the root in each of these words.

1. unforgettable	6. disorderly	11. demobilize
2. guitarist	7. pressurize	12. certainty
3. uncertain	8. nonprofit	13. mismanagement
4. disable	9. hornless	14. indigestion
5. popularity	10. unfaithful	15. unquestionable

Suffixes. Add one of the following suffixes to each of the words below: -ment, -able, -ful, -ish, -ant, -er, -less.

1. regret _____	5. grate _____	9. prefer _____
2. export _____	6. assort _____	10. joy _____
3. imp _____	7. unthink _____	11. enjoy _____
4. expect _____	8. heart _____	12. forget _____

Persuade and Convince

Obviously, a man's judgment cannot be better than the information on which he has based it. Give him the truth and he may still go wrong when he has the chance to be right; but give him no news or present him only with distorted and incomplete data, with ignorant, sloppy or biased reporting, with propaganda and deliberate falsehoods, and you destroy his whole reasoning processes, and make him something less than a man.

ARTHUR HAYS SULZBERGER

From a speech by Arthur Hays Sulzberger to the New York State Publishers Association, August 30, 1948.

Parts Department: Suffix Review

Write the correct form of the new word.

1. replace + able _____

2. submit + ed _____

3. lace + y _____

4. allot + ment _____

5. hope + ful _____

6. plan + ed _____

7. confer + ence _____

8. benefit + ing _____

9. gossip + y _____

10. appear + ance _____

11. marriage + able _____

12. plane + ing _____

Sound Sense: The ô Sound

Say these words: cl<u>aw</u>, p<u>au</u>se, t<u>a</u>ll, w<u>a</u>lk. The pronunciation key in the dictionary shows that each of the underlined letter combinations stands for the sound of ô. In the words below, underline the letter combinations that stand for the sound of ô.

1. draw	11. lawn	21. falcon	31. balance
2. pal	12. haul	22. wallet	32. falsify
3. fawn	13. aunt	23. malady	33. halibut
4. laugh	14. dawn	24. walnut	34. cauliflower
5. thaw	15. away	25. talcum	35. altitude
6. chalk	16. gauze	26. salmon	36. sausage
7. vault	17. balk	27. palace	37. nautical
8. talk	18. ballet	28. alcohol	38. rawhide
9. sauce	19. caught	29. caution	39. laundry
10. ball	20. gauge	30. gallery	40. calendar

Sound Sense: The Sounds of G

The letter g can stand for two sounds: a soft sound and a hard sound. When g is followed by e, i, or y, it usually has a soft sound, as in *general*, *giant*, or *gymnasium*. When g is followed by a, o, or u, it has a hard sound, as in *game*, *gold*, or *gulf*.

Identify the sound of g in the words below. Put H in the blank if the g has a hard sound; put S if it has a soft sound.

___ 1. gallop	___ 5. corsage	___ 9. origin	___13. refuge
___ 2. angel	___ 6. engulf	___10. fragile	___14. geology
___ 3. organ	___ 7. nostalgia	___11. goiter	___15. huge
___ 4. gypsum	___ 8. pagoda	___12. gyration	___16. bargain

Sound Sense: The Sounds of W

The letter w can stand for a consonant sound or for a vowel sound. Say these words:

wonder   wage   beware

When w begins either a word or a syllable, it is always pronounced and is considered a consonant. Now say these words:

new   coward   bawl

In these words w is combined with another vowel to form a special sound and is considered a vowel.

Identify the sound of w in the words below. Put C in the blank if the w stands for the consonant sound; put V if the w stands for the vowel sound.

___ 1. beware	___ 6. witch	___11. swing	___16. waste
___ 2. worth	___ 7. coward	___12. prowl	___17. claw
___ 3. crown	___ 8. wild	___13. flew	___18. wink
___ 4. knew	___ 9. rowdy	___14. worry	___19. chow
___ 5. waffle	___10. wad	___15. cowboy	___20. between

Key Words

dispensing-giving out; *consumption*-the amount used up

More Air Than Corn

Movie-goers are paying for a lot more air in their popcorn these days than in grandfather's time, a popcorn machine executive says. Special processing and equipment puff the kernel up to 40 times its original size, according to John C. Evans, vice-president of a Cincinnati firm, whose company claims to be the nation's largest popcorn-machine maker.

As a result, a quart-sized box of popcorn in movie houses holds only about one ounce of corn. But popcorn dispensing is still a half-billion-dollar industry, with consumption standing at an average of 2.2 pounds a year for every American. (95 words)

True or False

Mark each statement either true (T) or false (F).

___ 1. The Cincinnati firm is the nation's largest maker of popcorn.

___ 2. On the average, each American buys 2.2 pounds of popcorn each year.

___ 3. Each kernel of corn is puffed up to 40 times its original size.

___ 4. Popcorn dispensing is a five-hundred-million-dollar industry.

___ 5. The author implies that the customer is getting less corn for his money than he did years ago.

Would You Believe?

The word *kernel* comes from an old English word, *cyrnel*, made up of the root word *cyrn* (corn) and *el* (small).

Sound Sense: The Sounds of Y

The letter *y* can stand for a consonant sound or for a vowel sound. Say these words:

yellow   young   beyond

When *y* is at the beginning of a word or syllable, it stands for a consonant sound. Now read these words:

deny   myth   myself

When *y* is in the middle or at the end of a word or syllable, it stands for a vowel. When *y* stands for a vowel sound, it has two sounds, much like the short and long sounds of other vowels. For example:

system (short)   sky (long)   story (short)

In the words below, write C above the *y*'s that stand for consonant sounds, and V above *y*'s that stand for vowel sounds.

hymn   youth   canyon   hurry   cyanide   yoke

lyre   cycle   year   yarn   synonym   anybody

Key Words

exclusive–not shared with others; convenience–a thing that saves time or work

Something for Everyone

We build them for you—the taxpayer, the home owner, the leisure seeker. Millions of our profit dollars have been put to work to build new dams and to create lakes for your enjoyment and your comfort. All of our lakes are open for your pleasure, whenever conditions permit. We've built roads for you to get there, campsites for when you arrive, and thousands of acres of nature's wonderlands for your exclusive use.

When you're at home, isn't it good to know that our investments in your leisure and pleasure are furnishing you with at-home comfort, good lighting, and power to operate every convenience?

The next time you visit one of our beautiful lakes, relax and enjoy it. And remember us. We're the ones who thought of you when we created those lakes for your comfort and fun. (138 words)

Check It

Place the letter of the best answer in the blank.

___ 1. The above paragraphs are probably a) a story about lakes and dams, b) a description of camping grounds, c) an advertisement for a power company.

___ 2. If this *were* an article written by a power company, the power it claims to produce would be a) natural gas for the home, b) electrical power for the home, c) water for the home.

Parts Department: Contractions

Many times words are contracted, or joined, in a shortened form. *Don't* is a contraction for the two words *do* and *not*. The apostrophe (') takes the place of the letter or letters left out. Below is an exercise to test your skill with contracted forms. Half the exercise calls for writing the words that form the contraction; the other half requires you to write a contraction for two words.

1. isn't   _____ _____

2. _____ you   will

3. haven't   _____ _____

4. _____ shall   not

5. _____ they   are

6. you've   _____ _____

7. I'm   _____ _____

8. _____ will   not

9. he's   _____ _____

10. _____ it   was

11. couldn't   _____ _____

12. _____ can   not

13. it's   _____ _____

14. _____ they   will

15. _____ you   are

16. _____ never

17. she'd   _____ _____

Figures of Speech

A figure of speech is a word or expression having a meaning other than its literal (original, or exact) meaning. When Shakespeare writes, "Lend me your ears," or someone says after a meal, "I really made a pig of myself," neither means what he actually says. But think how much less effectively the writer gets across his meaning when he simply says, "Listen to me," or "I ate too much." The two most used figures of speech are *similes* and *metaphors*.

1. *Simile*. Often used in describing or explaining something, the simile points out a likeness between two objects by using a connective word. This connective word is usually *like* or *as*. An example of a simile would be, "He is *as cross as a bear* today," or "She ran *like a deer*."

2. *Metaphor*. People use metaphors when one thing reminds them of another. Like the simile, metaphors compare, but without using the *like* or *as*. The man who says of another, "He is *a sly fox*," is using a metaphor to compare a man's slyness to that of a fox. Forms in nature often suggest metaphors. Such wildflower names as "Dutchman's breeches," "jack-in-the-pulpit," and "bleeding heart" are good examples. In "The Highwayman," the poet Alfred Noyes sees a road at night as "a ribbon of moonlight." The Bible contains many nature metaphors, such as: "I am *the Vine*, ye are *the Branches*."

In the following exercises, underline the metaphor or simile in each of the sentences and write either S or M in the blank.

___ 1. Old Mr. Kingston's heart was a stone, hard and immovable.

___ 2. The operator's voice was like sandpaper, rasping and coarse.

___ 3. The crevice, like an open grave, seemed to beckon to me.

___ 4. All the world's a stage.

___ 5. Joe was a pillar of strength in his community.

___ 6. To me my home is the center of the universe.

___ 7. The old people were like lost children as they wandered through the streets.

___ 8. As my head struck the boulder, the pain was like an overwhelming wave sweeping over me.

___ 9. He is a tiger at the office but a lamb at home.

Words You Need

Read each sentence and choose the meaning of the word in italics. Write the letter of your answer on the line. Use your dictionary if necessary.

Place the letter of the correct answer in the blank.

___ 1. Praise will always *stimulate* most people to work harder.
Stimulate means a) assist; b) arouse; c) teach; d) calm.

___ 2. *Thermal* underwear has greatly aided the comfort of our troops in Alaska.
Thermal means a) cold; b) warm; c) strong; d) weak.

___ 3. Please *convey* my thanks to your father when you see him.
Convey means a) define; b) carry; c) hint; d) demonstrate.

___ 4. The *anarchists* wanted to overthrow the government so that there would be no ruling authority in the country.
An *anarchist* is one who a) seeks to rule; b) rebels against any authority or established order; c) is in favor of absolute order.

___ 5. Sunshine and moisture are *beneficial* to plants.
Beneficial means a) harmful; b) powerful; c) helpful; d) official.

___ 6. A clever *propagandist* can bring many votes for himself by means of the Glittering-Generalities Device.
Propagandist means one who a) opposes; b) spreads opinions in order to influence people; c) is indifferent; d) counts votes in an election.

___ 7. After two school buildings were destroyed, the police finally caught the boys responsible and put an end to their senseless *vandalism*.
Vandalism means a) willful destruction; b) treachery; c) setting fires; d) play.

___ 8. People have a *tendency* to yawn when they are sleepy.
Tendency means a) passion; b) natural urge; c) desire; d) need.

___ 9. He formed his own *deduction* about who raided the icebox when he saw the ice cream on his daughter's face.
Deduction means a) misunderstanding; b) question; c) answer to a problem, based on facts; d) disillusionment.

___10. The joke was so *subtle,* it took a while to get it.
Subtle means a) honest; b) simple; c) clever; d) dull.

Propaganda: How It Works and Why We Buy It

Part I

(1) Abraham Lincoln first made the famous remark, "You cannot fool all the people all of the time." Propagandists would like to try, though. They want to put something across and make people believe it without question. In this way they hope to bring about a particular effect. The effect may turn out to be beneficial or harmful to millions of people—this is why it is necessary to be able to recognize propaganda and understand how it operates.

(2) Propaganda has sold everything from popcorn to presidents. Propaganda is universal. Propagandists are all around us: authors, editors, advertisers, politicians, teachers, as well as our own friends and parents! They all want to influence us to believe and do certain things. *Words* are their tools—words loaded with emotion, such as "love," "hate," "honor," "duty," "home." We react to the feelings that these words arouse in us, and we usually believe and do what the propagandist hoped we would.

(3) We are affected by propaganda chiefly because we don't recognize it when we see it. Propaganda devices usually work most effectively, therefore, when we are too lazy or unsuspecting to think for ourselves. These devices appeal to our emotions rather than to our reason. They make us believe and do something we might not otherwise believe or do if we thought about it calmly and examined the evidence. Propaganda can govern our feelings for or against anything from war, education, freeways, and student power, to vitamins, king-size cigarettes, toothpaste with sex appeal, and no-cal cola. For

instance, a beautiful Hawaiian girl on television tells us that "*everyone* can afford Hawaii this year," and we run to our travel agent. Devices like this are clever, and they have changed very little over the years. A list of them, published in 1937 by the Institute for Propaganda Analysis, still applies today:

1. The Name-Calling Device
2. The Glittering-Generalities Device
3. The Transfer Device
4. The Testimonial Device
5. The Plain-Folks Device
6. The Card-Stacking Device
7. The Bandwagon Device

(4) The propagandist uses the device of Name-Calling to make us form quick judgments. He appeals to our emotions of hate, fear, and mistrust by giving "bad names" to certain individuals, nations, races, policies, and ideas which he wants us to condemn and reject. You will surely recognize some of today's "bad names": *extremist, radical, warmonger, communist, racist, anarchist, pig, square, fink.* How often have you heard these words lately? How often have you used them?

(5) Any political campaign abounds with Name-Calling. Often, instead of coming right out and referring to his opponent by name, an act which can lead to a lawsuit, a politician will try to link his opponent with such "bad name" groups or organizations as *anarchists, bureaucrats, racists,* and *extremists.* This is a subtle device to capitalize on the basic human emotions of fear and suspicion. The propagandist knows that if he keeps associating his rival's name with the "fat cats in City Hall" or the "racists," people will start believing that the candidate *must* be a racist or a "fat cat" himself. The more often the "bad names" are heard, the more believable they become. The propagandist has accomplished his aim—he ends up getting our votes.

(6) Pick up your daily newspaper and you will find it filled with Name-Calling propaganda. On the front page you may read about a campus riot in which students are reported to have complained about "police brutality." If the newswriter

happens to dislike the local police force, the student vandalism that went on will be played down, while whatever action the police took will be greatly exaggerated. A light scuffle between one policeman and one picket may be reported as "The police brutally threw hundreds of students to the ground."

(7) By using the Glittering-Generalities Device, a good propagandist can make us buy any idea. He uses words that suggest shining ideals, such as *truth, democracy, honor, duty, success, justice.* To our ears, these words stand for good things. The propagandist identifies his own race, nation, program, or belief with these "virtue" words to make us accept his views without question.

(8) The politician who identifies his campaign with the slogan "A Return to Law and Order" is using a Glittering Generality to make us vote for him. He knows that *law and order* are words that appeal to all races and classes of people. He takes advantage of the fact that there is no set, agreed-upon definition for *law and order.* What *order* means to one group may mean something entirely different to another. Most people don't bother to notice that the candidate may use few if any concrete examples of things he plans to do to bring about his idea of law and order. Few people bother to examine the candidate's background to see what his previous stand on law and order has been. The "glitter" glosses things over and pulls in the votes.

(9) How often have you heard a news announcer say something like this: "Informed sources have it that the war is taking a turn in our favor now"? *Informed sources* has a ring of authority and accuracy, doesn't it? It glitters. The news announcer wants you to think that you are receiving the best, most reliable news. Have you ever really questioned who the *informed sources* are? The news that is finally broadcast has gone through many channels before it reaches the public. One must realize that reporters and newswriters have a human tendency to work their own ideas into a news story and are likely to make their own deductions from press-conference remarks. Many people tend to believe that the *informed sources* are actually the president, the commanding general at the front,

or a mysterious all-knowing "they" in Washington. Often the source turns out to be a jeep driver the reporter befriended on his way to the front.

(10) Why have the beasts of the jungle suddenly become so popular with today's car buyer? Why do we want a wildcat under our hood and a tiger in our tank? Propagandists know that symbols such as these stir up our emotions and stimulate exciting mental pictures of raw, naked fury when we press the accelerator. So, by using this Transfer device, the propagandist uses the cat's qualities of sleekness, power, and speed to sell us the latest set of wheels.

(11) The label "Approved for the U.S. Olympic Team" has been very successful in selling everything from thermal underwear to bathing suits. Most people have great respect and admiration for Olympic athletes. When they see that a product is considered good enough for the Olympic team, most people buy. The non-commercial image of the Olympics also helps sell the product by leading people to believe that the price must therefore be absolutely fair. Thus, by means of the Transfer device, the respect which people have for Olympic teams is transferred to the product for sale.

(12) The familiar figure of Uncle Sam in a tall hat and striped trousers is a favorite propaganda tool of political cartoonists. For example, if a cartoonist wants to show disapproval of proposed legislation that would lower the voting age, he may draw a picture of Uncle Sam frowning at under-age voters. Because Uncle Sam represents "all that is wise, just, and good," the propagandist can thus convey the impression that the country is unquestionably against the bill, and it might well be defeated. This is an often-used example of a national symbol being used as a Transfer device in propaganda, and it is particularly successful. (1264 words)

Time:_____

Check It Place the letter of the correct answer in the blank.

___ 1. A political cartoon showing Uncle Sam would be an example of a) the Transfer Device; b) the Name-Calling Device; c) the Bandwagon Device.

___ 2. Propagandists use our _____ to make all of their devices work. a) emotions; b) memories; c) love.

___ 3. All propaganda is a) bad; b) good; c) neither *a* nor *b*.

___ 4. By means of the Transfer Device, people's _____ can be transferred to a product for sale. a) doubt; b) respect; c) fear.

___ 5. We are sometimes fooled by propaganda because we a) don't recognize it; b) believe it; c) are afraid.

___ 6. One good place to find examples of all the propaganda devices would be in a) a newspaper; b) TV commercials; c) either *a* or *b*.

___ 7. The Name-Calling Device appeals to our a) insecurity; b) hate and fear; c) love for mankind.

___ 8. As propaganda devices, Name-Calling and Glittering Generalities a) stir up emotion; b) fog our thinking; c) both *a* and *b*.

Sound Sense: W and Y Review

Identify the sounds of *w* and *y* in the words below. Put C in the blank if the *w* or *y* stands for a consonant sound; put V if the *w* or *y* stands for a vowel sound.

___ 1. mysterious	___ 6. upward	___11. typical
___ 2. howl	___ 7. shallow	___12. dye
___ 3. awful	___ 8. yelling	___13. weave
___ 4. young	___ 9. watch	___14. happy
___ 5. wiggle	___10. view	___15. yacht

Words You Need

Read each sentence and choose the meaning of the word in italics. Write the letter of your answer on the line. Use your dictionary if necessary.

Place the letter of the correct answer in the blank.

___ 1. I will make a *prediction* about when the next earthquake will be.

Prediction means a) prophecy (or forecast); b) decision; c) agreement; d) warning.

___ 2. A dishonest salesperson will try to *dupe* customers by selling them poorly made merchandise.

Dupe means a) please; b) fascinate; c) sell; d) deceive.

___ 3. Mary *blithely* signed the contract without reading the small print.

Blithely means a) quietly; b) carefully; c) casually.

___ 4. People believed the movie star's *testimonial* that the new diet food was good for one's health.

Testimonial means a) lie; b) examination; c) statement about benefits received from something; d) court statement.

___ 5. Being a football player and a wrestler is, to some, the image of strength and *virility.*

Virility means a) cowardice; b) muscles; c) virtue; d) manliness.

___ 6. The little boy *invaded* his sister's privacy when he entered her room without knocking.

Invade means a) take away; b) deny; c) burst in upon; d) surround.

___ 7. It is *crucial* that you pass this test if you want to graduate.

Crucial means a) nice; b) unimportant; c) effective; d) extremely important.

___ 8. You must *evaluate* carefully what you read in the newspaper, for much of what you read is opinion, not fact.

Evaluate means a) look at; b) understand; c) examine carefully and judge.

___ 9. The king ordered his men into battle, seeking *vengeance* on the country that had kidnapped his son.

Vengeance means a) pity; b) revenge; c) anger; d) a curse.

___10. Many people *evade* unpleasant topics by changing the subject.

Evade means a) lengthen; b) avoid; c) seek; d) follow.

Propaganda: How It Works and Why We Buy It

Part II

(13) Our TV is being invaded almost hourly with friendly housewives chanting, "I use Sparkle in my washing machine and I can *see* the difference! My sheets are whiter, colors are brighter." Why are we seeing so many ads like this on TV today? Because they *work*. This Testimonial Device is one of the most effective techniques in advertising. A housewife likes to hear from another woman just like herself that a new detergent, hair spray, or aspirin *really* works. The woman-to-woman effect of the ad makes the viewer feel that she can trust what is being said.

(14) But the women are not alone. The men are meanwhile tuning in on locker-room conversations like this:

(15) "What do you use after a shave, Bob?" says sports announcer Al Perkins to Bob Dragore, star of the Green Bay Packers.

(16) "I use Zing. It makes my skin feel cool, refreshed. And I like the smell," replies Bob, as he examines his shave in the mirror.

(17) Such interviews are selling lots of after-shave lotion these days. The testimonial of the star quarterback has the ring of authority. He is a symbol of virility and masculinity, and he transfers these qualities to the product he advertises. People subconsciously think to themselves, "If someone like him uses it, it must be OK." Zing therefore sells because men are made to feel that anything said in a locker-room man-to-man talk with Bob Dragore must be on the level.

(18) Why do politicians kiss babies? Why do they invade kitch-

ens to sample apple pies, shoot pool at the neighborhood pool hall and wipe out on a surfboard? Because they know they will get more votes if people think they are "just plain folks" like you and me, and therefore *must* be honest and good. This Plain-Folks Device is very popular with businessmen. Top executives in steel companies often don hard hats and personally inspect their mills to be "plain folks" with the men who work the furnaces. These executives speak the slang of the mill with the men. They ask questions about jobs, families, and homes. This is an excellent way to make workers feel important; that their jobs are being noticed by the men at the top.

(19) Does "Mother's Brick-Oven Bread" sound good to you? Why? The word *Mother's* adds something special to the bread, doesn't it? In our minds we see a picture of golden, fresh-baked loaves being taken out of a brick oven by a plump, rosy-cheeked mother. Mother is a Plain-Folks symbol. She is good, honest, and down-to-earth, just like any other mother. People buy Mother's Brick-Oven Bread because they feel that Mother would use only the finest ingredients—no shortcuts for her. She would serve only the freshest, richest bread. However, if you stopped to think about it, you'd realize that the "Brick Oven" is probably a huge factory two blocks long!

(20) Propagandists often use the Card-Stacking Device in order to make their arguments sound more convincing. Suppose a group of citizens in your town is supporting a law that would set a ten o'clock curfew for anyone under eighteen. Their main argument is: Statistics show that eighty percent of the criminal activity in this town occurs after ten P.M. Perhaps the cards are being stacked against the truth here; important facts may be left out. Statistics don't lie, but it is questionable if they can prove as much as people claim they can prove. First of all, what *kind* of criminal activity are we talking about? Traffic accidents? Loitering? How much of the eighty percent involves people *over* eighteen? Over how long a period of time does this statistic apply? Many people, not bothering to realize how little this statistic supports the argument, will blithely sign the petition.

(21) An agent trying to sell a house tells a young couple, "You'll have peace and quiet out here for sure, far away from the freeways. This house you could really feel *settled* in. Two-car garage, full basement. Schools close by. For this price, you can't afford *not* to take it." This salesman is a Card-Stacker. He knows that the government is soon going to build a four-lane superhighway right in front of the house, and the garage is "two-car" only if you have two cars hardly bigger than motorized scooters. The "full" basement floods every time it rains, and the nearby schools are very poor. This salesman's propaganda contains no outright lies; it merely evades the truth by omitting such superfluous details as the new super-highway.

(22) Nobody likes to be a drag. It's much easier, and much more fun, to go along with the crowd, to "jump on the band-wagon." By means of the Bandwagon Device, propagandists get people to do something by making them believe that *every-one else* is doing it. For example, a successful car dealer may run a TV ad that sounds like this: "Everyone is getting in on the big year-end sale of this year's model. Join the crowds. Come on down." Pictures of huge crowds rushing to the car agency are flashed upon the screen. This type of ad has a very powerful effect on the viewers. People begin thinking, "If all those people are rushing down to that sale, the prices really must be low. *I* can afford it if everyone else can." The band-wagon rolls on.

(23) "We've got Arizona, we've got Colorado, we've got Texas, and now it's time for *this* great state to become part of that ever-growing crowd that knows a winner when it sees one!" This politician is using the Bandwagon Device to appeal to the basic human desire to follow the crowd. He builds up emotions to a fever pitch in order to win the voters to his side. When people are caught up in the movement of the crowd, they usually jump on the bandwagon without really thinking about it. There are probably lots of bandwagons around your school and neighborhood. Perhaps you yourself have hopped on one recently.

(24) Many football games are "won" in midweek when team

leaders make predictions such as this: "We're going to win. No question. It's in the bag. We've got *three* quarterbacks better than the Bombers' star quarterback." Besides annoying the enemy, propaganda like this can pep up the underdog team and give it the confidence needed to win. This Prediction Device is not confined to the sports world only, but some of the best examples of it are found there. For example, the press may spread the "We're going to win" prediction all over the sports pages in an effort to beef up interest in the game. By means of this propaganda, a whole new tide of feeling sweeps over the players and fans alike. When sports fans read that the underdog Jays fully expect to beat the Bombers, rumors fly, the odds start shifting, and bets change. As game time draws closer, emotions take over. The favored Bombers are angry. The Jays don't even belong in the same league, they feel. The Jays' quarterbacks are nothing special. The Bombers lose their professional poise and vow to get even with the Jays, especially with the player who made the prediction. They ignore the fact that this vengeance will cost them crucial misjudgments in the game. If the Jays can capitalize on this, the propaganda has done its work well.

(25) None of us likes to be duped. We like to know what is really going on; we need to know, therefore, *when* propagandists are working on us. As we have seen, propagandists are all around us, trying to sell us on many different things. We should be alert to propaganda's signals and many clever disguises. Because we are human, though, propagandists will always be able to work on us through our emotions. How successful these propagandists will be depends entirely on us—upon how well we evaluate and examine what we see and hear around us. (1319 words)

Time:_____

Check It

Place the letter of the correct answer in the blank.

___ 1. The main idea of this article is that the public needs a) to accept propaganda; b) to be critical of advertisements; c) to be aware of propaganda devices.

___ 2. The Testimonial Device leads people to believe they are hearing _____ about a product for sale. a) a rumor; b) the real truth; c) a lie.

___ 3. Propagandists use the Card-Stacking Device to make their arguments sound more a) illogical; b) convincing; c) pleasant.

___ 4. The Plain-Folks Device is used by executives to make workers feel a) ignored; b) plain; c) important.

___ 5. The propagandist does not want you to _____ his propaganda too closely. a) support; b) examine; c) follow.

___ 6. A prediction of victory by an underdog team may cause the opposing team to a) quit; b) become angry and play poorly; c) play another team.

___ 7. The Bandwagon Device appeals to our desire to a) be the first person to buy the new product; b) hear the inside story on a new product; c) go along with the crowd.

___ 8. When he uses the Plain-Folks Device, the propagandist tries to appear a) different from us; b) outstanding; c) just like ourselves.

___ 9. Card-stackers often _____ the truth. a) tell; b) evade; c) question.

Name some kinds of propaganda that you meet at school, at work, and at home. _____

_____

_____

_____

Abbreviations in the Dictionary

Abbreviations and symbols are used extensively in the dictionary in order to save space. Notice the number of abbreviations and symbols used in this entry.

folk (fōk), *n.* [*pl.* FOLK, FOLKS (fōks)], [ME.; AS. *folc;* akin to G. *volk;* IE. base **pel-,* to fill (prob. specialized < **pel-,* to pour, flow), seen also in Eng. *full,* L. *plere,* to fill up, *plenus,* full (cf. PLENUM), *plebs,* the common people (cf. PLEBEIAN), *populus,* people, nation (cf. PEOPLE, POPULAR), redupl. < **po-pel-os;* basic sense prob. "crowd"], 1. a people; race; tribe; nation; ethnic group. 2. *pl.* people; persons: as, *folks* don't agree, town *folk* are not like farmers. *adj.* of or existing among the common people: often distinguished from *art,* as, *folk* ballads differ from art ballads.

Somewhere in your dictionary you should find a page listing the abbreviations and symbols used. You need to become familiar with this page and develop the habit of using it.

Here are some of the abbreviations and symbols that appear in one dictionary. Use them to help you read the entry for *folk* (above) and to work the following exercise.

Symbol	Meaning				
<	derived from	**dial.**	dialect	**ML.**	Medieval Latin
*	hypothetical	**dim.**	diminutive	**n.**	noun
+	plus	**Eng.**	English	**OFr.**	Old French
?	perhaps, uncertain	**Fr.**	French	**ON.**	Old Norse
		G.	German	**orig.**	origin, originally
adj.	adjective	**Gr.**	Greek		
AS.	Anglo-Saxon	**IE.**	Indo-European	**pl.**	plural
c.	century	**It.**	Italian	**prob.**	probably
cf.	compare	**L.**	Latin	**redupl.**	reduplication
colloq.	colloquial	**lit.**	literally	**Sw.**	Swedish
D.	Dutch	**LL.**	Late Latin	**transl.**	translation
		ME.	Middle English		

Abbreviations and symbols are used most frequently in etymologies. Write these etymologies, spelling out all abbreviations and symbols. The first one is done for you.

1. boulder [< *boulder stone;* ME. *bulderstan* < ON.; cf. Sw. *bullersten,* lit. noise stone]

Derived from <u>boulder</u> <u>stone;</u> Middle English <u>bulderstan</u> derived

from Old Norse; compare Swedish <u>bullersten,</u> literally noise stone.

2. centipede [< Fr., L *centipeda* < *centum* a hundred +*pes, pedis,* a foot]

_____

_____

3. cellophane [< *cellulose* +Gr. *phaein* to appear, seem]

_____

_____

4. muscle [< Fr.; L. *musculus,* a muscle, lit. little mouse, dim. of *mus,* a mouse]

_____

_____

5. nasty [ME. *nasty, nasky, naxty;* ? < or akin to D. *nestig,* dirty; or ? < ON.; cf. Sw. dial. *naskug,* foul]

_____

_____

6. derrick [after Derrick, London hangman of the early 17th c. orig. applied to a gallows]

_____

Parts Department: Prefixes of Number

There are many prefixes that indicate *number*. For instance, *bicycle* tells you that there are *two* cycles (or wheels) on your machine. Here is a list of the most common prefixes that stand for numbers:

uni-, mono-	: one	sept-	: seven
bi-, di-, du-	: two	oct-	: eight
tri-	: three	novem-	: nine
quad-	: four	dec-	: ten
pent-, quint-	: five	cent-	: hundred
sex-, hex-	: six	hemi-, semi-	: half

Fill in the blanks in the following sentences with the correct number.

1. Under the Roman calendar, September was the _____ month of the year.

2. A bigamist is one who has married _____ persons.

3. A three-sided figure is called a _____angle.

4. One tone would be a _____tone.

5. There are _____ parts to a duplex.

6. In a sextet, there are _____ people.

7. The Pentagon in Washington, D.C., has _____ sides.

8. A century is _____ years, but a decade is only _____ years.

9. An octopus has _____ arms.

10. A quadruplet is one of _____ children.

They Work to Win

Athletes as a rule are stronger than their backers; yet the weaker presses the stronger to put forth all his efforts.

St. Jerome/Letter 118

Key Words

<u>consolidated</u>–combined; <u>unconscious</u>–not aware of

---

The Future Is Now

To the girl swimmers from California's golden land the future always looks good, perhaps because they have sheltered themselves so from the present. They come from where the hot winds blow and the divorce rate far exceeds the national, where one person in 38 lives in a trailer, and where the misplaced children from broken homes gather. But for the girls there are only the blue pools filled season into season. They will go through the consolidated high schools, and nobody will ask them out for Saturday night's dance or the drive-in movie and a burger on The Strip, because they have no time. Swimming is their life, and they are unconscious of all but its demands. You wonder why they go to all those practices.

It is no wonder, really. It is an Olympic year, and all these girls are too young to have even known any other Olympics. From the time they first splashed through a race, this is the one thing, the one year, they have been after. "Olympic medals are the real reward," says Debbie Meyer, "in my line of work." (185 words)

From "The Only Year of Their Lives." Reprinted in part by permission from *Sports Illustrated,* August 12, 1968 © 1968 Time Inc.

True or False

Mark each statement either true (T) or false (F).

___ 1. The girl swimmers are very much a part of the present.

___ 2. Each girl has had experience in several Olympic contests.

___ 3. The swimmers are unpopular with other students.

—— 4. Each girl is working toward a goal of winning medals.

—— 5. The writer implies that the girls are not aware of life in the communities around them.

Sound Sense: The SCHWA Sound

Say each of these words, noting the sound for which the underlined vowel stands:

about   lion   elephant   alone   agent

Did you notice that the underlined vowel sounds the same in each word and that in each word that vowel is in an unaccented syllable? This vowel sound is called a *schwa*. In the dictionary, it looks like this: ə (ə bout). Say each word below and underline each vowel letter that stands for the schwa sound.

pilot   ago   student   razor   pleasant
oblige   mystery   lesson   human   comma

Parts Department: Prefixes of Number Review

Fill in the blanks to complete these sentences.

1. Monoxide has _____ atom of oxygen in each molecule.

2. _____focals are glasses with two different focal lengths.

3. In a duet there are _____ persons involved.

4. It is said that a _____pede has a hundred feet.

5. A _____syllabic word has three syllables.

6. A quarter literally means _____ equal parts of something.

7. A pentadactyl pertains to something having _____ fingers or toes on each hand or foot.

8. In music an octave consists of _____ tones.

Key Words
marine–of the sea; species–a distinct kind; anglers–those who fish with a hook and line; simultaneously–at the same time; predatory– preying on other animals

Of Parks and Fish

(1) Point Reyes National Seashore on California's northern coast has more than 50 miles of hiking trails. The trails wind through coastal forests and beautiful meadows where wildflowers abound in the spring. Horseback riding is permitted on all the trails, and the Bear Valley and Coast trails are suitable for bicycling. Three campgrounds are available for backpackers. Tide pools at McClure's Beach support a wide variety of marine life. In addition, over 300 species of birds and 72 species of animals inhabit this coastal area. Visitors can picnic, swim, do surf fishing, and take four self-guiding nature study trails. Rock hounds can explore a site where the 1906 earthquake exposed rocks of two distinctly different types and ages. The Point Reyes National Seashore is truly a paradise for nature enthusiasts.

(2) In many cases the practice of transplanting fish from one geographic area to another works to the benefit of good sport fishing. For example, striped bass were transplanted from the Atlantic Coast of North America to the Sacramento Delta in California. When the fish make their annual run up the coastal rivers, they provide anglers with challenging excitement. People in Wyoming can catch record-size California golden trout, which were transplanted to the Wind River Mountains area. Rainbow trout, originally native to Western North America, are now found all over the world. On the other hand, when Atlantic salmon and American smelt were introduced simultaneously into the Great Lakes (the latter as a food source for the more valuable salmon), the salmon didn't sur-

vive. The predatory smelt soon wiped out species of smaller fish and overpopulated the lakes. Likewise, carp from Asia that were planted in many parts of this country as game fish have proved to be a nuisance because they destroy the eggs of other fish. In some cases, then, the practice of transplanting fish has hindered the enjoyment of sport fishermen. (314 words)

Check It

Underline the main idea in each of the above paragraphs.

Sound Sense: Homonyms

Words that are pronounced alike but are spelled differently and have different meanings are called homonyms (from a Greek word, *homonymos: homos*, same + *onyma*, name). Writers often have problems with homonyms because they must remember the correct spelling of the word needed. Write homonyms for each of the words below.

1. fair _____   5. pair _____

2. flee _____   6. new _____

3. quire _____   7. for _____

4. pain _____   8. bowl _____

Underline the homonym that correctly completes each sentence.

9. We are going to have a long (weight, wait) for the next flight.

10. You just (past, passed) my mom's office on your way here.

11. The children listened with (rapped, wrapped, rapt) attention.

12. Senator Brown is very (vein, vane, vain).

13. The players remained (stationery, stationary) most of the time.

14. Mr. Allan is the (principle, principal) speaker.

15. Marilyn is the (sole, soul) owner of this business.

16. The sick man answered (weekly, weakly).

Key Words
concern–interest in; *inject*–introduce

Hooked on Sports

Anyone who reads an American newspaper is surely convinced that sports are among the major activities and interests of our people. When international news items are crowded off the front page by headlines that give the latest score on a World Series game, there's positive proof that Americans are willing to set aside their concerns for the state of the world for who's pitching in the eighth. There are tens of millions of people who take their sports in the grandstands or in front of a television set, but there are also tens of millions of others who spend their weekends on the golf course, in motor boats, on mountain slopes, or in the bowling alleys.

Sports touch most of our lives, and for some they are a means to social and economic success. They influence the design of clothing and automobiles, they create heroes overnight, and they even inject new and fascinating words into our language. Millions of dollars are circulated each year, simply because millions of people want to watch and to participate in major and minor sports. No matter what an individual may think of sports, they're a vital part of the American way of life. (199 words)

True or False

Mark each statement either true (T) or false (F).

___ 1. Most people are more interested in international affairs than they are in sports.

___ 2. Sports are for both spectators and participants.

___ 3. An athlete can lose his social status when he participates in sports.

___ 4. Sports have little influence on newspaper reporting.

___ 5. It is implied that sports represent big business in America.

Parts Department: Compound Words

Read the following sentence: Everywhere you look in the schoolyard, everyone is playing with a basketball. Can you find four compound words in that sentence? Compound words are a combination of two or more words in which the spelling does not change and the meaning becomes a combined meaning of the parts. Some compounds are not actually written together (post office, ice cream) and a few are still written with hyphens (son-in-law, one-half). Draw a line separating the parts of these compound words:

anyone	something	baseball	roommate
bookkeeper	nobody	homework	anything

Can you add other compound words to the list?

Figures of Speech: Personification and Hyperbole

Personification is a figure of speech in which lifeless objects are given qualities of living things. For example, ships, locomotives, autos, and airplanes are generally spoken of in terms of the pronoun *she*. We may use adjectives, as in *the angry sea, the thirsty ground*. Or, we may have lifeless objects or qualities performing life-like actions, as in "The old moon *laughed*," and "Happiness *bubbled over*."

In order to impress you, a writer may use a hyperbole, a figure of speech which uses deliberate, and often outrageous, exaggeration. Example: "Waves high as mountains broke over the reef," or "I am so hungry I could eat a horse."

In the following sentences underline the word or words that indicate either personification or hyperbole. Write P or H in the blank.

___ 1. Hunger stalked the village, touching every family.

___ 2. I was so embarrassed I was ready to die on the spot.

___ 3. The abandoned factory building looked forlorn and lifeless.

___ 4. Fortune smiled and sheltered our family during the storm.

___ 5. Henry was so angry he looked ready to burst.

___ 6. I spent so much money this week we'll live on beans the next six months.

___ 7. Death lays his icy hands on kings and commoners alike.

___ 8. Opportunity knocks at least once at every door.

___ 9. Jack Frost poked his icy fingers through the thin blanket which covered the dying man.

___10. Tim felt so confident he was ready to take on the troubles of the whole world.

Words You Need

Read each sentence and choose the meaning of the word in italics. Write the letter of your answer on the line. Use your dictionary if necessary.

___ 1. *Cricket* is one of the favorite games in the British Isles.
   In this sentence, *cricket* means: a) a sport; b) a small black insect; c) to be honest.

___ 2. The impact of the crash *hurtled* the driver against the wheel.
   In this sentence, *hurtled* means: a) injured; b) dashed violently; c) pulled.

___ 3. We watched a *spectacular* display of fireworks at the fair.
   In this sentence, *spectacular* means: a) bright; b) eye-catching, dramatic; c) long distance.

___ 4. John was so *absorbed* in his studies that he didn't hear the telephone ring.
   In this sentence, *absorbed* means: a) wrapped up; b) soaked up; c) swallowed up.

___ 5. In the *fateful* battle most of Napoleon's soldiers were killed.
   In this sentence, *fateful* means: a) loyal; b) long and tiring; c) disastrous.

The Flying Scot

The red and gold Lotus-Ford came out of the treacherous "Shrimp's Head" curve and blasted down the straightaway on the rain-slick track. Running seventh in the first of two heats, Jimmy Clark was pushing the Lotus at what later was estimated as a speed of 175 miles per hour. Then it happened. The Lotus swung sideways on the track and hurtled into the trees facing the track. When the officials reached him, Jim Clark was dead of a broken neck and multiple fractures. The force of the speed of the out-of-control Lotus had smashed it against a tree. There wasn't enough left of the car to learn why the accident had occurred. The shy Scotsman, who lay crumpled on the soft floor of the forest, had once said, "The one thing a driver fears is a mechanical fault in his car—something which is not under his control. You never doubt your own ability. But when there is any doubt about what the car is going to do it really unnerves you." Jimmy Clark, considered by many to be the world's outstanding racing driver, had, on that fateful day of April 7, 1968, ended his colorful career. The place was Hockenheim, West Germany. The car that Jimmy drove had been tested only twice before. Graham Hill, one of Jimmy's best friends and fellow drivers, had tested it at Silverstone for 200 miles, and he had found the car in perfect shape. But the crash that day in Hockenheim was not Jimmy Clark's fault. Something must have gone wrong in the Lotus-Ford—something that was not under Jimmy's control.

Anyone who loved good cars and skillful drivers was shocked and saddened by the news of Jimmy's death. He had been the youngest driver ever to win the Grand Prix, when in 1963 he took the checkered flag for seven races. He was only twenty-seven, and he was World Champion.

It would almost seem that Jim Clark was born to be a racer. At the age of nine, he took his father's Austin Seven and drove it around the farm. His father hadn't given him permission to use the car, of course, and Jim knew an excitement that he had never felt before. In fact, he could not have known on that day that within a few years he would become one of the world's finest racing drivers.

Jim was born on a farm in Fife County, Scotland, on March 4, 1936. His parents, James and Helen Clark, were quiet, hard-working people. When Jim was only six, his father bought the big farm across the Firth of Forth at Edington Mains, in Berwickshire.

The young boy grew up learning everything he could about taking care of farm animals. He was sent to a fine school, but he was more interested in rugby and cricket than he was in his studies. So, when he was sixteen, Jim was brought home to the farm and put to work herding the sheep at Edington Mains. That's when he started thinking about racing cars.

Jim's first car was an old Sunbeam Talbot, and he drove it in local rallies through the Scottish countryside. There he learned to drive between points that had been set up by the other boys. He had to maintain a certain speed in order to finish the rally in a specified time.

"That Jim has all the makings of a good driver," said one of his friends as he watched Jim flash by in the Sunbeam Talbot. "He drives with his head. Nothing seems to excite him."

Mr. Clark wasn't very excited about Jim's driving. He had dreams of Jim's becoming master of Edington Mains, and when his son was only eighteen years old, Mr. Clark and the rest of the family moved to another farm that was owned by the Duke of Roxburgh. Jim was left at Edington Mains to run the farm by himself. At eighteen, Jim felt that running the farm was quite a responsibility.

It was in 1956, when Jim was twenty years old, that he

started changing tires and helping drivers at the Border Reivers, a Scottish auto racing club. One day he was helping Ian Scott Watson, a fine driver.

"Why don't you take the wheel, Jim?" asked Watson.

Jim eased himself gently into the DKW (Das Kleine Wunder, or the Little Wonder) sedan. With a roar, he was off. When he returned to the starting point, he had made his lap in three seconds faster than Watson's best time. Watson was looking at Jim with wonder.

"You'll make a fine racing driver, Jim," said Watson, slowly. "You've got just what it takes."

Jim was wearing a dark blue crash helmet that Watson had given to him. Until his very last race, Jim wore that blue helmet. It was almost like a trademark, but it also served to remind him of the Border Reivers where he got his start in racing.

In 1958, Jim Clark finished in first place and won the Scottish speed championship. Two years later, he won the British championship and ranked eighth in world standings. It was then that he knew for sure that he would always be a driver. And, other drivers knew that they had someone to contend with in the cool young Scotsman.

There was just one thing that stood in Jim's way, however. That was Edington Mains. His father had left him in charge, and Jim really loved the farm. He knew that the farmers around him talked about how he neglected the farm. But he also knew that he could farm and race, too. When he left the farm for a race, he always left it in the good hands of his helpers.

To win the Grand Prix is the ambition of nearly every racing driver. Since 1950, the person who has won the Grand Prix has been known as the World Champion.

Jim Clark wanted to win the Grand Prix. He had become such a good driver that companies wanted him to drive their cars. Jim drove in a lot of races, but he never quite made the championship. He would return to Edington Mains and the very next year he would be driving again.

Something happened in 1961 that almost caused Jim to give

up driving. He was competing at Monza, Italy, and he was driving a Lotus for Colin Chapman. Chapman had worked on a new design for his Lotus, and it was far from perfect. He knew, however, that he had one of the best drivers for his Lotus when Jim Clark was at the wheel.

The race was on, and Jim was handling the Lotus as only he could. As he swept over the course, he could feel the excitement of the large crowd that had gathered to watch the race. Near him was a driver in a Ferrari, a man whom Jim respected very much, Wolfgang von Trips. Then it happened.

Wolfgang von Trips swerved his Ferrari in front of Clark's Lotus. Both cars were going over 150 miles an hour. In a split second, Jim knew that they were going to crash. The Ferrari touched the Lotus, and then it was completely out of control. Up the bank the Ferrari hurtled. It struck and tore out a long part of the fence. In a matter of seconds, fifteen people who were standing near or leaning on the fence had been killed. The Ferrari rolled back on the track. Wolfgang von Trips was dead inside the smashed Ferrari.

That was not the first time that Jim Clark had seen an accident on the race tracks. In fact, he knew that any driver was bound to see accidents and that he must be prepared to be hurt himself. But nothing that Jim had experienced before was as horrible as that accident at Monza. One of his good friends was dead, and all of those other people had been killed. When Jim returned to Edington Mains, he was a very sad young man.

That night Jim walked out and stood under the stars and looked across his land. Everything was so quiet and peaceful. Here on the farm there was no great violence, no danger of death at the wheel. Jim had won a lot of races, but he was not sure that night that he wanted to race again.

Of course, there was a lot of talk among the neighbors. None of them thought that Jim would race again, and there were some of them who thought that Jim should not race again. They watched Jim as he went quietly about his business of running the farm.

Three days later, Jim was packing his bag for another race.

"When a thing like that happens, you vow you will never drive in a race again," he said. "I was lucky to have been blessed with a short memory."

In 1962, Jim Clark was behind the wheel again. He was determined to win the Grand Prix. That was the greatest of all honors to come to a driver, and Jim felt that he could win it. Certainly he had failed before, but so had others. He was ahead in the competition until the final race in South Africa. Then his oil supply began leaking. Graham Hill nosed him out for the championship.

When Jim won the Grand Prix in 1963, he became the youngest driver ever to win it. He won seven of the races, the greatest number that any driver had ever won. In the Belgium Grand Prix, he had held a loose gear lever with one hand while he had steered with the other. He had competed against some of the finest drivers in the world, and he had finally won the Grand Prix!

Jim lost his crown in 1964 to John Surtees. It was a hard race to lose. He was on the last lap of the season's last race in the Mexican Grand Prix when his crankcase went dry. But in 1965 it was Jim Clark, World Champion, again! That time he won a race that he had wanted to win since he had begun racing, the German Grand Prix. For the first time, people saw Jim Clark really excited. When the race was finished, he grinned and said, "I'm as happy as a king. This is the one that was missing!"

There was one great race that Jim had never won. That was the Indianapolis Memorial Day 500. In 1963, he came in second to Parnelli Jones. In 1964, the tread peeled off a tire when he was going 150 miles per hour, and he was out of the race entirely. Then came 1965, Jim's greatest racing year. He had qualified for the Indianapolis race in early May, driving a hot new engine, a 500 horsepower Lotus-Ford with a rear engine.

It was a bright day when the thirty-two qualified cars roared away from the starting grid at Indianapolis. A. J. Foyt was ahead on the first lap, and he was a hard man to beat. By the end of the second lap, Jim was ahead of Foyt and he was clocked at 151.38 miles per hour, a new track record. From then on, it was Clark's race all the way. At the end of the race, only ten cars remained on the track. Twenty-two cars had dropped out, many of them scattering pieces as they left the track. Foyt was out with his transmission gone. As he passed the finish line, Clark raised his hand in salute to the crowd, and the people roared with joy. Jim had shown them a spectacular job of driving. He had clocked a record 150.68 miles per hour for the entire race, the fastest time ever to be driven at Indianapolis. As people roared and as friends pounded Jim on the back, he grinned calmly. "You know," he said, "there were never any real tense moments out there."

What made Jim Clark such a good driver? Many sports writers watched him drive, and they thought he was the world's greatest. He had excellent vision, a fine sense of timing, and he always appeared to be under excellent control. No one ever saw Jim angry. One time he said, "If you let your feelings go, you'll be dangerous to yourself. The car happens to be under me and I'm driving it, but I'm a part of it and it's a part of me."

Jim Clark was a quiet, gentle young man. He didn't drink and he didn't smoke. He liked to listen to both classical and jazz music. He was both a driver and a farmer. You could see him, between races, moving about Edington Mains taking care of his farm. His Scottish sheep dog, Sweep, was always by his side.

Perhaps Jim learned something that most people never learn. He was satisfied with himself as he was. He liked himself as a farmer, and he gained great satisfaction from working at Edington Mains. When he drove a racing car, he was one of the best, completely absorbed in his car. He once said, "If you're a Scot, you don't push yourself forward. That's the way I was brought up."

And that's the way he was until the very end, on that fateful day when his car went out of control in Hockenheim on a rain-slick track. Jimmy was buried on a chilly but sunny day in a tiny stone church at Chirnside, only a few miles from the place he loved best—his farm in Scotland. (2259 words)

Time:_____

Check It

Write the letter of the best answer in the blank.

___ 1. The main idea of this article is that

    a) anyone can be a good driver if he works hard.

    b) Jim Clark had unusual qualities as a driver.

    c) winning the Grand Prix requires courage.

___ 2. Jim Clark's greatest conflict with himself was

    a) how to remain a good driver and be honest, too.

    b) how to be a good farmer and a driver, too.

    c) how to win enough racing money to support his farm.

___ 3. When Jim Clark drove his father's Austin Seven,

    a) he knew that one day he'd be a great driver.

    b) he was planning to be one of the world's great drivers.

    c) he could not have known that he'd become a great driver.

___ 4. Jim returned to Edington Mains after his races

    a) to take care of the cattle and sheep.

    b) to maintain a balance within himself.

    c) to convince the neighbors that he was a good farmer.

___ 5. Jim's father wasn't excited about his son's driving career

    a) because he feared Jim would be killed.

    b) because he feared what the neighbors might think.

    c) because he wanted his son to become master of the farm.

___ 6. Jim Clark knew for sure that he always wanted to be a driver when

    a) he drove Watson's DKW.

    b) he won the Scottish speed championship.

    c) he won the British championship.

___ 7. When Jim said, "I was lucky to be blessed with a short memory," he meant that

    a) he had forgotten about the death of his friend.

    b) he could not remember the ugly part of racing.

    c) he could continue to race but not entirely forget von Trips' death.

___ 8. Which statement best describes Jim Clark?

    a) He was quiet, frequently angry, but controlled.

    b) He was quiet, gentle, and perfectly controlled.

    c) He was determined to win at any cost.

Box Scores

```
NEW YORK            PHILADELPHIA
         ab r h bi              ab r h bi
Linz 2b   6 3 5 3  Rolas 2b     3 0 0 0
CJones lf 6 1 4 3  Brown p       0 0 0 0
Swoboda rf 6 0 1 0 Joseph ph     1 0 0 0
Charles 3b 2 1 1 0 Farrell p     0 0 0 0
Collins 3b 5 1 0 1 Callison ph   1 0 0 0
Grote c    4 1 2 0 James p       0 0 0 0
Goossen 1b 4 0 1 0 Pena ss       5 1 2 0
Agee cf    1 0 0 0 Gonzalez cf   5 2 2 0
Shamsky lf 2 0 1 1 RAllen lf     3 1 0 0
Bosch cf   0 1 0 0 Lock rf       4 1 3 4
Weis ss    4 2 1 1 TTaylor 3b    4 1 2 0
AJackson p 4 1 2 1 Briggs 1b     4 0 0 1
RTaylor p  0 0 0 0 Ryan c        4 0 2 0
WShort p   0 0 0 0 Fryman p      1 0 0 0
Kranpool ph 1 0 0 0 Wagner p     0 0 0 0
Koonce p   0 0 0 0 Hall p        0 0 0 0
                   Sutherlnd 2b  3 0 2 1

Total    40 11 18 10  Total    38 6 13 6
New York ....... 0 2 1 0 3 0 0 2 3—11
Philadelphia .... 2 0 0 0 0 0 0 4 0— 6
DP—New York 1, Philadelphia 1. LOB—
New York 10, Philadelphia 7. 2B—
Gonzalez 2, Lock, Linz, Shamsky,
C.Jones. S—Goossen, Collins. SF—
Shamsky, Collins.
                    IP   H  R ER BB SO
A.Jackson (W,2-3) . 7    9  4  4  1  1
R.Taylor .......... 2-3  4  2  2  0  0
W.Short ........... 1-3  0  0  0  0  0
Koonce ............ 1    0  0  0  0  0
Fryman (L,10-9) ... 2    8  3  3  1  1
Wagner ............ 2 2-3 4 3  3  1  0
Hall .............. 1-3  0  0  0  0  1
Brown ............. 2    1  0  0  1  1
Farrell ........... 1    2  2  2  0  0
James ............. 1    3  3  3  1  0
HBP—Wagner (Charles).
T—3:03. A— 4,032.
```

Baseball box scores in the sports section of a newspaper present special reading problems. First, examine the box score and the key to the abbreviations. Then answer the questions below.

A	attendance	L	loser
2B	two-base hit	lf	left field
2b	second base	LOB	left on base
ab	at bat	ph	pinch hitter
BB	base on balls	r	runs
rbi	runs batted in	S	sacrifice
DP	double play	SF	sacrifice fly
ER	earned runs	SO	strikeouts
H	hits	ss	shortstop
HBP	hit by pitcher	T	time
IP	innings pitched	W	winner

1. Who played third base for New York? _____

2. Who was Philadelphia's catcher? _____

3. How many hits did Weis get? _____

4. How many times was Pena at bat? _____

5. How many double plays were made in the game? _____

6. How many doubles were hit? _____

7. How many innings did Wagner pitch? _____

8. How many strikeouts did Brown get? _____

9. What is the winning pitcher's record? _____

A Matter of Record

MID-OHIO TRANS-AMERICAN

Date: June 11, 1967
Course: 2.4 miles

Site: Mid-Ohio Sports Car Course, Lexington, Ohio
Race distance: 125 laps, 300 miles

Pos.	Driver	Car	Class	Qual. Time	Qual. Speed	Start Pos.	Laps
1.	Jerry Titus	Mustang	O-2	1:46.8	80.90	2	125
2.	David Pearson	Cougar	O-2	1:46.4*	81.20*	1	125
3.	George Follmer	Camaro	O-2	1:49.8	78.69	7	122
4.	Horst Kwech	Alfa Romeo GTA	U-2	1:53.2	76.33	11	120
5.	Jim Baker	Alfa Romeo GTA	U-2	1:56.6	74.10	22	119
6.	Craig Fisher	Camaro	O-2	1:52.8	76.60	10	119
7.	Bert Everett	Porsche 911	U-2	1:55.4	74.87	19	118
8.	Roger West	Camaro	O-2	1:55.0	75.13	15	118
9.	John Kelly	Porsche 911	U-2	1:56.6	74.10	23	116
10.	Dick Hoffman	Camaro	O-2	1:57.2	73.72	24	111
11.	John McComb	Mustang	O-2	1:54.4	75.52	14	111
12.	Fred Opert	Porsche 911	U-2	1:58.0	73.22	25	109
13.	Don Sesslar/Freddy Van Beuren	Mustang	O-2	1:48.8	79.41	4	109
14.	Milt Minter	Mustang	O-2	1:50.2	78.40	8	106
15.	Tony Adamowicz	Lotus-Cortina	U-2	1:56.4	74.23	21	100
16.	Gene Henderson	Lotus-Cortina	U-2	1:58.6	72.85	26	70
		DID NOT FINISH					
17.	Monte Winkler	Alfa Romeo GTA	U-2	1:53.6	76.06	12	116
18.	Dwight Knupp	Barracuda	O-2	1:55.6	74.74	20	100
19.	Don Hamilton	Camaro	O-2	1:54.2	75.83	13	92
20.	Ed Leslie	Cougar	O-2	1:47.0	80.75	3	77
21.	Jim Adams	Mustang	O-2	1:48.8	79.41	5	53
22.	Bernd Leckow	NSU 1000	U-2	2:06.2	68.46	31	39
23.	Herb Swan	BMW-TISA	U-2	2:05.6	68.79	30	36
24.	Pete Feistmann	Mustang	O-2	1:51.4	77.56	9	32
25.	Tom Payne	Lotus-Cortina	U-2	2:02.6	70.44	27	30
26.	Gary Morgan	Camaro	O-2	1:55.2	75.00	16	28
27.	Bob Tullius	Dodge Dart	O-2	1:55.2	75.00	17	27
28.	Jim Brown	Rambler	O-2	2:02.8	70.36	28	26
29.	John Moore	Camaro	O-2	1:55.4	74.87	18	21
30.	Charlie Rainville	Barracuda	O-2	2:07.2	67.92	32	16
31.	Dick Sorenson	Lotus-Cortina	U-2	2:03.2	70.13	29	8
32.	Allan Moffat	Mustang	O-2	1:49.2	79.12	6	disq.

* New lap record.

Race time: 3h, 54m, 51.2s. **Winner's average speed:** 76.664 mph.
Fastest race lap: Jerry Titus, 1:48.8 (79.416 mph — new record).
Lap leaders: David Pearson 1; Jerry Titus 2-125.

After reading the chart above, answer these questions.

1. How many drivers finished the race? _____

2. What was the total distance of one lap? _____

3. What was the total distance of the race? _____

4. Who established a new lap record? _____

5. How many of the drivers who started in the first five positions completed the race? _____

6. Where was the race run? _____

7. What was the total time for the race? _____

8. What was the fastest qualifying speed? _____

9. What kind of a car did the winner drive? _____

10. What was the starting position of Charlie Rainville? _____

11. Who was the only driver in a Rambler? _____

12. What driver drove the most laps before being forced out of the race? _____

Sound Sense: Schwa Review

Underline the vowels that stand for the schwa sound in these words.

1. gallop	11. riot
2. memory	12. escalate
3. control	13. legal
4. dolphin	14. oppose
5. random	15. arise
6. balance	16. Siamese
7. salmon	17. cotton
8. consonant	18. opossum
9. direct	19. fungus
10. common	20. fundamental

Would You Believe?

Although English is the basic language in both England and America, there are some differences among the words that are used to mean the same thing. Try to match the British expression with the American word in the lists below.

___	1. petrol	a.	radio
___	2. biscuits	b.	hood
___	3. lift	c.	wrench
___	4. stalls	d.	crackers, cookies
___	5. holiday	e.	elevator
___	6. bonnet	f.	gasoline
___	7. fortnight	g.	windshield
___	8. lorry	h.	orchestra seats
___	9. maize	i.	garbage collector
___	10. windscreen	j.	vest
___	11. spanner	k.	vacation
___	12. dustman	l.	corn
___	13. waistcoat	m.	newsstand
___	14. kiosk	n.	truck
___	15. wireless	o.	two weeks

Men Apart

8

Incident

Once riding in old Baltimore,
    Heart-filled, head-filled with glee,
I saw a Baltimorean
    Keep looking straight at me.

Now I was eight and very small,
    And he was no whit bigger,
And so I smiled, but he poked out
    His tongue, and called me "Nigger."

I saw the whole of Baltimore
    From May until December;
Of all the things that happened there
    That's all that I remember.

COUNTEE CULLEN

Key Words
functions-duties, proper work; _media_-newspapers, magazines, TV, etc.; _embrace_-include, contain

Changing Beliefs About Women

There is no one definition of feminine behavior and character. In some cultures the women are the hard workers; in others the men are. In some cultures pregnancy and children are resented; in others pregnancy and children are idealized.

To a great extent each culture determines sex roles in its own way and sets its own standards. Some common notions that we have believed in our own culture are that women are inferior to men, that women are the attractive and beautiful sex, and that women are to do all the feeding and caring functions in the society. We have learned these ideas from our families and schools and through the media.

Today, however, these ideas are being challenged, and women are being thought of in new ways. Descriptions of behavior and feelings that were once considered feminine may no longer be true. Women are being defined differently, and the new definitions embrace a broader view about what women are and can be than ever before. Today, women are demanding and getting the right to change their life-styles. (179 words)

True or False

Mark each statement either true (T) or false (F).

____ 1. Women are now interested in changing their roles.

____ 2. In certain cultures there are definite roles defined for women.

____ 3. Time-honored roles for women will never change.

Parts Department: The Syllable

A syllable is a word or word part in which you hear only one vowel sound. Read the words below and notice how many vowels you see in each word. Then say the words aloud and write above each word the number of vowel sounds you *hear* in that word. For example: careful.

1. come   goat   November   mysteriously   pen   begin

Now complete this statement:

2. A word has as many syllables as it has _____sounds.

As you can see, when vowels are silent in a word, they do not form syllables. Draw a line through the silent vowels in the words below. Then, above each word, write the number of syllables in that word. For example: become

3. sheeting	12. door
4. approach	13. crossroads
5. moment	14. royalty
6. caterpillar	15. finally
7. microscope	16. succeed
8. yesterday	17. allocate
9. drain	18. reporters
10. threesome	19. careful
11. amusing	20. geography

Key Words
compel–to force; prosper–to succeed

Appeal to Justice

Chief Joseph

Treat all men alike. Give them the same law. Give them an even chance to live and grow. All men were made by the same Great Spirit Chief. They are all brothers. The earth is the mother of all the people, and all people should have equal rights upon it. You might as well expect the rivers to run backwards as that any man who was born a free man should be content when penned up and denied liberty to go where he pleases. If you tie a horse to a stake, do you think he will grow fat? If you pen an Indian up on a small spot of earth and compel him to stay there, he will not be contented, nor will he grow and prosper. I have asked some of the great white chiefs where they get their authority to say to the Indian that he shall stay in one place, while he sees white men going where they please. They cannot tell me. (167 words)

True or False
Mark each statement either true (T) or false (F).

___ 1. Men of different races need different laws.

___ 2. All men have the same creator.

___ 3. The white men had good reason for treating the Indians as they did.

___ 4. The white chiefs explained their authority by referring to their laws.

___ 5. The author implies that the Indian cannot survive on reservations.

Reading an Encyclopedia

One important source of information is the encyclopedia. Knowing how to read an encyclopedia correctly can save you valuable time, and lead you to important information. Examine carefully this entry taken from *The World Book Encyclopedia*.

RACING

Guide words, as in your dictionary, help you locate entries quickly.

Entry topic in bold face type helps find topics quickly.

Internal cross references indicate sources of related information in other encyclopedia articles.

Sub-headings help you find major divisions of the entry topic.

RACING is a trial of speed in running, rowing, swimming, riding, driving, flying, or any other physical activity with two or more participants.

Contests of speed of both men and animals have excited keen interest from the earliest times. The successful runner in the early Greek games was crowned with a wreath of laurel, and was honored by all the people. Various kinds of racing games were also popular with the people of ancient Rome.

In modern times, contests of speed have become a regular part of the rivalry among colleges, especially in the United States and Canada. The Olympic Games, held in ancient times, are popular in their revived modern form. They include many races, among them the famous marathon run. See OLYMPIC GAMES; TRACK AND FIELD (table).

Man has invented machines that give him greater speed. Bicycle, motorcycle, automobile, and airplane races were added to trotting, pacing, and running races as popular sports. Automobile racing is one of the most exciting sports because of the great speeds reached by the drivers. Many persons also enjoy the thrill of sailing and rowing races (see ROWING). Bicycle racing was once a rival of horse racing in America. Although it has lost some of its popularity, it is still a favorite amateur sport. For many years before World War II, the six-day bicycle race was one of the chief sports attractions in the United States. In Europe, especially in Italy, France, and Belgium, bicycle racing is a major sport. Important races are held every year. The famous races Tour of France and Tour of Italy cover more than 2,000 miles each.

Dog Racing has been a sport since the days of ancient Egypt. The chief dogs used for racing are the Saluki (an Egyptian breed), the greyhound, and the whippet (see GREYHOUND; WHIPPET). There are only about 30 American dog tracks, but these have great popularity. England is the most important dog-racing country in the world, and each year the famous greyhound race for the

From *The World Book Encyclopedia*. © 1969 Field Enterprises Educational Corporation.

Parts Department: Combining Forms

Combining Form	Prefix or Suffix	Meaning	Complete Word
auto (self)	mobile (s.)	_____	automobile
	graph(y) (s.)	_____	autograph
	crat (s.)	_____	autocrat
cide (causing death)	sui (p.)	_____	suicide
	geno (p.)	_____	genocide
	homo (p.)	_____	homocide
hydro (water)	acoustic (s.)	_____	hydroacoustic
	meter (s.)	_____	hydrometer
	pathy (s.)	_____	hydropathy
manu (hand)	fact(ure) (s.)	_____	manufacture
	script (s.)	_____	manuscript
	duct(ion) (s.)	_____	manuduction
scope (view, look)	tele (p.)	_____	telescope
	micro (p.)	_____	microscope
	stetho (p.)	_____	stethoscope

Parts Department: The Vowel Syllable

Remember that a word has as many syllables as it has vowel sounds. Sometimes a vowel may form a syllable by itself. Say these words. Write 1, 2, or 3 beside each word to show how many syllables it contains. Underline a vowel if it forms a syllable by itself.

1. about _____

2. indicate _____

3. elephant _____

4. through _____

5. prepare _____

6. lion _____

7. again _____

8. violet _____

9. related _____

10. hexagon _____

Parts Department: Roots

Listed here are five words formed from the root *port*. Study the word parts carefully and then complete the sentences below with words from the list.

porter   *port*, carry + *er*, a person who

import   *im*, in, into + *port*, carry

transport   *trans*, across + *port*, carry

deport   *de*, away + *port*, carry

portable   *port*, carry + *able*, capable of being

1. The big, heavy television set was not _____.

2. The shipping company was asked to _____ the wheat across the ocean.

3. Jane wanted to _____ a car from Europe.

4. At the train depot, a _____ took our luggage.

5. Because of the man's criminal record, the government decided to _____ him from the country.

Key Words
myth-a legend or story; *primitive*-simple, uncivilized

The Myth of Race

Ashley Montagu

The idea of "race" represents one of the most dangerous myths of our time, and one of the most tragic. Myths are most effective and dangerous when they remain unrecognized for what they are. Many of us are happy believing that myths are what primitive people believe in, and that we ourselves do not believe in myths. We may realize that a myth is an incorrect explanation leading us to believing something wrongly, but we do not usually realize that we ourselves share in myth-making with all men of all times and places, that each of us has his own store of myths which have been derived from the traditional stock of the society in which we live. In earlier days we believed in magic, possession, and exorcism, in good and evil supernatural powers, and until recently we believed in witchcraft. Today many of us believe in "race." "Race" is the witchcraft of our time. The means by which we drive away demons. It is the contemporary myth. Man's most dangerous myth. (172 words)

True or False
Mark each statement either true (T) or false (F).

__ 1. A myth is a faulty explanation leading to a belief.

__ 2. Myths can be dangerous.

__ 3. The idea of "race" is an ancient myth.

__ 4. Today most people don't believe in the myth of "race."

__ 5. The author implies that we must eliminate the myth of "race" from our thinking.

Parts Department: Accented Syllables

Remember that a word has as many syllables as it has vowel sounds, and sometimes a vowel forms a syllable by itself. A dictionary always shows how to divide a word into syllables. The diagonal line shows the one syllable that is *accented*, or spoken with more stress than other syllables in the same word:

cer'•tain   def•i•ni'•tion

Say the following words. Mark the syllable that is accented.

1. teach er
2. con grat u late
3. fa ther
4. be gin
5. grad u a tion
6. trans por ta tion
7. un hap py
8. mar vel ous
9. be gin ning
10. a bove

Irony, Oxymorons, and Puns

Irony is a figure of speech in which the ordinary meaning of the words is the opposite of the thought in the speaker's mind. Or it may refer to an unexpected ending when we are first given facts that point to an expected result. Irony is from a Greek word that means "to cover up" or "to hide." Examples: In his speech over Caesar's body, Antony talks about the "honorable" men who have stabbed Caesar. (He really meant they were dishonorable.) A stunt man who survives falls from cliffs, stagecoaches, and tall buildings arrives home only to step on his son's skate and break his leg. (This unexpected ending is ironic.)

Oxymoron is a figure of speech in which words of opposite meaning or suggestion are used together. Examples: a wise fool; cruel kindness; to make haste slowly. It comes from the Greek word *oxys*, meaning "sharp," and *moros*, meaning "stupid."

A pun is a play on words which have the same sounds but

different meanings. Examples: "Is life worth living? That depends upon the liver." "We must all hang together, or we shall all hang separately."—B. Franklin

In each blank write I, O, or P to show whether the sentence contains irony, oxymoron, or a pun.

___ 1. Sweet revenge was the motive of the gruesome crime.

___ 2. After months of drought, the farmers finally finished digging a canal to bring water from a lake five miles away; a week later it rained.

___ 3. Why don't you shut your mouth, dear!

___ 4. "O sweet pain" is an expression from *Romeo and Juliet*.

___ 5. The stumbling blind man picked up a hammer and saw.

___ 6. A week after I had pawned all my valuables to purchase a second-hand car, I won a beautiful Cadillac at a drawing!

___ 7. Bill yelled to Tom, "You lie like a rug!"

___ 8. The townspeople felt pity for the poor little rich girl who had all the wealth in the world but was suffering from malnutrition.

___ 9. Your well-mannered son just threw a rock through my front window.

___10. Some hippies are well-heeled although they wear no shoes.

Would You Believe?

Many words have changed meaning as time has passed. Today you might describe a person as being *cunning, silly,* or *pretty.* Using your dictionary, find out what these words meant when they were first used in the language.

1. cunning _____

2. silly _____

3. pretty _____

Words You Need

Read each sentence and choose the meaning of the word in italics. Write the letter of your answer on the line. Use your dictionary if necessary.

___ 1. That the sun will rise tomorrow is *inevitable*.
Inevitable means a) necessary; b) unavoidable; c) useless.

___ 2. On the rebellious campus, much *extremist* talk was heard.
Extremist means a) farthest from the political middle; b) moderate; c) discouraging.

___ 3. A *plurality* of the students voted for the third choice of no homework over the weekend.
Plurality means a) equal number; b) majority; c) greatest number.

___ 4. It is *apparent* that the days become longer in June.
Apparent means a) not known; b) difficult to see or understand; c) easy to see or understand.

___ 5. The *ingredients* of a simple salad are vegetables, hard-boiled eggs, and a tangy dressing.
Ingredients means a) food; b) parts of a mixture; c) combined mixture.

___ 6. The mother *segregated* the sick child so that the other children wouldn't catch his measles.
Segregated means a) hospitalized; b) kept apart; c) placed together.

___ 7. Many students attend private *academies* instead of public schools.
Academies means a) buildings; b) places of learning; c) gatherings.

___ 8. The police had to deal *drastically* with the vandals to put a stop to the crime wave.
Drastically means a) leniently; b) indifferently; c) forcefully.

___ 9. A child has *reliance* on his parents.
Reliance means a) dependence; b) fear; c) distrust.

___10. Several schools voted to form a *unified* school district.
Unified means a) separate; b) different; c) united.

Some Uncomfortable Questions

Loudon Wainwright

(1) How much does the ordinary white man really want to see the Negro as his equal? How much is he ready to give; how much will he personally help to see the Negro gain a better place in society? In short, what can he do?

(2) Perhaps these questions are not concerned so much with the white American's conscience as with his ability to see what is going on around him. For there is a revolution in progress; its outcome—the fulfillment of Negro hopes for the power of full citizenship—is inevitable. The only choices remaining to white or black are about methods, the choice of violence or non-violence, resisting the revolution or joining it. I think some people still cling to the wishful and ridiculous notion that the whole thing can be solved without much cost to them. Somehow, they hope civil rights bills, gifts of money, and sympathy will "equalize" the Negro while leaving the white place in society unchanged.

(3) Surely, this kind of wishful thinking is almost as harmful to black-white understanding as the noisy anger of extremists of both races.

(4) The extraordinary gap between the white man's good intentions and his actual willingness to see that they are carried out is shown in a recent poll taken by Louis Harris. Of the whites questioned, a small plurality agreed with the idea that cities should be given enough money to rebuild slums. Yet most of these same people were against being taxed to pay for this rebuilding. Judging by the answers given to other questions, white Americans seem to have formed their own

opinions without regard to the findings of fact-seekers. By a two-to-one majority, they disagreed with the opinion of the president's Riot Commission that the 1967 riots were not organized. And with an apparent desire for revenge that seems astonishing, another majority flatly opposed the commission statement that people arrested during the riots should have gotten better advice from lawyers and fairer trials.

(5) Another Harris study shows truly disturbing changes in the feelings of Negro Americans in the midst of this revolution. Over a period of two years, the poll found the Negro's sense of separation from society had risen very sharply. In 1966, far fewer Negroes reported this feeling, but now real majorities believe that "few people really understand how it is to live like I live," or "people running the country don't really care what happens to people like ourselves," or "almost nobody understands the problems facing me." The fact that most of these same people also think that racial progress has increased in the past few years makes me think that there must be something very important missing in this progress.

(6) Surely one of these missing ingredients must be a new willingness to take positive, personal steps toward the goals of this revolution. Whites must not stand apart. It is widely accepted that one important "cooling" factor to New York's small outbreak of violence after the shooting of Dr. Martin Luther King was the sight, again and again, of Mayor John Lindsay in the streets of Harlem. To many who saw him, Lindsay's presence showed not only his courage but also his concern about the anger and confusion that Dr. King's murder had caused.

(7) Far more whites should be going into the ghetto communities and working there for the improvement of those places and their people. All too few are urged to leave the comfort of their segregated way of life and follow the example of the young white teachers who hold "street academies" for Harlem drop-outs. The physical presence of the white man in the ghetto is needed, not as shopkeeper or policeman, but as a person trying to understand "how it is to live like I live" and to help change drastically that life. Moreover, such actions

would certainly help wipe out the feelings of separation on the part of blacks.

(8) Since the death of Dr. King, many Negroes have acted to prevent a sudden rise in violence. There is evidence that the dreadful murder has finally shown people how terribly close we have come to total breakdown between black and white. Since then, Negroes have started a drive to put black candidates in office. Such reliance on the vote is far better than riots, but I wonder how far we've all come, if we're even close to the time when black and white will be truly unified. (738 words)

Check It   **Time:**_____

Place the letter of the correct answer in the blank.

___ 1. The title "Some Uncomfortable Questions" is so stated because
   a) the white man must ask of himself just how much he really wants to see the Negro as his equal.
   b) the questions are embarrassing to the Negro.
   c) the white man cannot answer questions about the Negro problem.

___ 2. Some white people still hope that problems of racial strife can be solved by
   a) complete suppression of the Negroes' demands.
   b) complete submission to the Negroes' demands.
   c) passage of civil rights bills and gifts of money.

___ 3. The intention gap refers to
   a) the differences in opinion between the whites and blacks.
   b) differences in opinion about the amount of money to be spent.
   c) differences between intentions and actuality.

___ 4. Among the whites who approved rehabilitation of slums, a poll showed that these same whites
   a) were for higher taxes for rehabilitation purposes.
   b) were not for higher taxes.
   c) voiced no opinion on financing.

___ 5. The Harris poll revealed a change in Negro sentiment which showed the Negroes' sense of alienation had

a) risen sharply.

b) decreased.

c) not changed.

___ 6. In New York's outbreak of violence after the assassination of Dr. Martin Luther King, one important "cooling" factor was

a) the repeated appearance of Mrs. Martin Luther King.

b) the world's recognition of Martin Luther King as a great man.

c) the repeated appearance of Mayor John Lindsay in Harlem.

___ 7. The author would like to see more whites

a) stay away from Negro ghettos.

b) actually live and work in Negro ghettos.

c) than Negro merchants and law enforcement officers in the ghetto.

___ 8. The aspiration of every Negro is

a) an opportunity for decent employment.

b) an opportunity for decent housing.

c) the enjoyment of the rights and privileges of full citizenship.

___ 9. The gap between intentions and reality can be minimized by

a) the Negroes' continual demand for racial equality.

b) government controls.

c) the white man's willingness for complete involvement.

___ 10. The reader might infer that the author

a) is skeptical about closing the intention gap.

b) is very optimistic about closing the intention gap.

c) feels that the intention gap can never be closed.

Reading an Encyclopedia

The information at the end of an encyclopedia entry can often be as important as the information found within the entry. Examine carefully the data found at the end of the entry, *Races of Man,* taken from *The World Book Encyclopedia.*

Related Articles list guides you to other articles that provide additional information on the topic.

Related Articles in WORLD BOOK include:

Africa (Racial Groups)	Cephalic Index	Malay
Ainu	Eskimo	Negrito
Aleut	Hamite	Negro
Asia (Races and Tribes)	Hottentot	Pygmy
Bushman	Indian, American	Samoyed

Outline gives breakdown of the contents of the article. It is valuable as a study guide before or after reading the article and can serve as a guide for note taking. It is really a table of contents of the article.

Outline

I. What Is a Race?
II. "Pure" Races
III. Caucasoids
IV. Negroids
V. Mongoloids
VI. Distribution of Basic Stocks
VII. Race Superiority
VIII. Race and Nationality

Questions

Nonwhite people make up what part of the earth's population?
What are the three principal races of man?
Most Europeans belong to what racial group?
How does race differ from nationality?
What are five principal physical characteristics of white people?
Why were Nazi leaders wrong in saying that the German people belonged to a "superior race"?
Why are Ethiopians sometimes called *Hamites?*
Can a biologist tell the cells of a German from those of a Chinese? Why?

Questions can be read before you read the article so that you don't miss major facts. Reread them afterward to test your learning.

RACHEL, *rah SHELL* (1820-1858), was a French actress. Born ÉLISA FÉLIX, of poor Jewish parents in Switzerland, she was found as a child singing in the streets of Paris. She studied drama at the Conservatory and made her debut at the Comédie Française in 1838. Her intensity and power in Jean Racine's *Phèdre* and other tragedies made her an international sensation. She died of tuberculosis. MARSTON BALCH

RACHEL, *RAY chul,* was the favorite wife of Jacob. Jacob served her father, Laban, seven years to win her, and his love was so great, "they seemed to him but a few days" (Genesis 29:20). But then Laban tricked him and gave him Rachel's older sister, Leah, instead. Jacob

From *The World Book Encyclopedia.* © 1969 Field Enterprises Educational Corporation.

Many encyclopedias also include book lists which will help you go beyond the information contained in the article. They will guide you to important works on the topic.

Words You Need

Read each sentence and choose the meaning of the word in italics. Write the letter of your answer on the line. Use your dictionary if necessary.

___ 1. When he climbed out of the escape tunnel, he *evaded* the guards and headed for the woods.

   Evaded means a) answered; b) avoided; c) attached.

___ 2. We had to *forfeit* the game when our bus broke down fifty miles from the ball park.

   Forfeit means a) give up; b) seize; c) tie.

___ 3. With his two jobs, family, clubs, and committees, he lived in a state of *ferment*.

   Ferment means a) surprise; b) peace; c) unrest.

___ 4. "Never do today what you can put off till tomorrow" is the theory of *procrastination*.

   Procrastination means a) cheating; b) delaying; c) dishonesty.

___ 5. The *cumulative* effects of the war—poverty, hunger, and displaced persons—were greater than the losses in the war itself.

   Cumulative means a) lasting; b) final; c) added.

___ 6. The yearly memorial service is designed to *perpetuate* the memory of our leader.

   Perpetuate means a) continue; b) end; c) destroy.

___ 7. It's difficult to be *rational* when you're angry.

   Rational means a) harsh; b) reasonable; c) calm.

___ 8. His *complacent* smile after scoring three goals angered the other players.

   Complacent means a) shy; b) hidden; c) self-satisfied.

___ 9. Citizens locked their doors as the *turbulent* mob advanced through the streets.

   Turbulent means a) happy; b) disturbed; c) large.

___10. The unhappy girl's forced smile gave an *illusion* of happiness.

   Illusion means a) false impression; b) happy sight; c) image.

A Testament of Hope

Martin Luther King, Jr.

Whenever I am asked my opinion of the current state of the civil rights movement, I am forced to pause; it is not easy to describe a crisis so profound that it has caused the most powerful nation in the world to stagger in confusion and bewilderment. Today's problems are so acute because the tragic evasions and defaults of several centuries have built up to disaster proportions. The luxury of a leisurely approach to urgent solutions was forfeited by ignoring the issues for too long. The nation waited until the black man was explosive with fury before stirring itself even to partial concern. Confronted now with the interrelated problems of war, inflation, urban decay, white backlash, and a climate of violence, it is now *forced* to address itself to race relations and poverty, and it is tragically unprepared. What might once have been a series of separate problems now merges into a complex social crisis.

I am not sad that black Americans are rebelling; this was not only inevitable but greatly desirable. Without this magnificent ferment among Negroes, the old evasions and procrastinations would have continued indefinitely. Black men have slammed the door shut on a past of deadening passivity. Except for the Reconstruction years, they have never in their long history on American soil struggled with such creativity and courage for their freedom. These are our bright years of becoming visible; though they are painful ones, they cannot be avoided. The sullen and silent slave of 110 years ago, an object of scorn at worst or of pity at best, is today's angry man. He is on the move; he is forcing change, rather than waiting for it. In less than two decades, he has roared out of slumber to change so many of his life's conditions that he may yet find the means to hasten his march toward and overtake the racing locomotive of history.

The price of progress would have been high enough at the best of times, but we are in a national crisis because a complex of profound problems has met in an explosive mixture. The black surge toward freedom has raised justifiable demands for racial justice in our major cities at a time when all the problems of city life have erupted at the same time. Schools, transportation, water supply, traffic, and crime would have been municipal agonies whether or not Negroes lived in our cities. We are unable at this moment to arrange an order of priorities that promises solutions that are decent and just.

Millions of Americans are coming to see that we are fighting an immoral war that costs nearly 30 billion dollars a year, that we are perpetuating racism, that we are tolerating almost 40,000,000 poor during an overflowing material abundance. Yet they remain helpless to end the war, to feed the hungry, to make brotherhood a reality; this has to shake our faith in ourselves. If we look honestly at our national life, it is clear that we are not marching forward; we are groping and stumbling; we are divided and confused. Our moral and spiritual values sink, even as our material wealth ascends. In this setting, the black revolution is more than a struggle for the rights of Negroes. It is forcing America to face all its flaws—racism, poverty, militarism, and materialism. It is exposing evils that are rooted deeply in the whole structure of our society. It suggests that radical reconstruction of society itself is the real issue to be faced.

Today there are fewer and fewer jobs for the culturally and educationally deprived; thus does present-day poverty feed upon itself. The Negro today cannot escape from his ghetto in the way that Irish, Italian, Jewish, and Polish immigrants escaped from their ghettos fifty years ago. New methods of escape must be found. And one of these roads to escape will be a more equal sharing of political power between Negroes and whites. Integration is meaningless without the sharing of power. When I speak of integration, I don't mean a romantic mixing of colors, I mean a real sharing of power and responsibility. We will eventually achieve this, but it is going to be much more difficult for us than for any other minority.

I have come to hope that American Negroes can be a bridge between white civilization and the non-white nations of the world, because we have roots in both. Spiritually, Negroes identify with Africa, an identification that is rooted largely in our color; but all of us are a part of the white-American world, too. Our education has been Western and our language, our attitudes—though we sometimes tend to deny it—are very much influenced by Western civilization. Although we are neither, in another sense we are both Americans and Africans. Our very bloodlines are a mixture. I hope and feel that out of the commonness of our experience, we can help make peace and harmony in this world more possible.

One of the most basic weapons in the fight for social justice will be the cumulative political power of the Negro. I can foresee the Negro vote becoming consistently the decisive vote in national elections. The party and the candidate that get the support of the Negro voter in national elections have a very definite edge, and we intend to use this fact to win advances in the struggle for human rights. For instance, the election of Negro mayors in some of the nation's larger cities has had a tremendous psychological impact upon the Negro. It has shown him that he has the potential to participate in the determination of his destiny—and that of society.

One of the most hopeful changes that has occurred is the attitude of the Southern Negro himself. Quiet acceptance of second-class citizenship has been displaced by vigorous demands for full citizenship rights and opportunities. In fact, most of our real accomplishments have been limited largely to the South. We have put an end to racial segregation in the South; we have brought about the beginnings of reform in the political system; and, as unbelievable as it may seem, a Negro is probably safer in most Southern cities than he is in the cities of the North. We have confronted the racist policemen of the South and demanded reforms in the police departments. We have confronted the Southern racist power structure and we have elected Negro and liberal white candidates through much of the South in the past ten years. There is a new respect for black votes and black citizenship that just did not exist ten years ago. Though school integration has moved at a depressingly slow rate in the South, it *has* moved. Of far more importance is the fact that we have learned that the integration of schools does not necessarily solve the inadequacy of schools. White schools are often just about as bad as black schools, and integrated schools sometimes tend to merge the problems of the two without solving either of them.

There *is* progress in the South, however—progress expressed by the presence of Negroes in the Georgia House of Representatives, in the election of a Negro to the Mississippi House of Representatives, in the election of a black sheriff in Tuskegee, Alabama, and, most especially, in the integration of police forces throughout the Southern states. So there *are* some changes, but the changes are basically in the social and political areas. The problems we now face—providing jobs, better housing, and better education for the poor throughout the country—will require money for their solution, a fact that makes those solutions all the more difficult.

The need for solutions, meanwhile, becomes more urgent every day, because these problems are far more serious now than they were just a few years ago. Before 1964, things were getting better economically for the Negro; but after that year, things began to take a turn for the worse. In particular, automation began to cut into our jobs very badly, and this snuffed out the few sparks of hope that black people had begun to nurture. As long as there was some measurable and steady economic progress, Negroes were willing and able to press harder and work harder and hope for something better. But when the door began to close on the few avenues of progress, then hopeless despair began to set in.

Solutions for these problems, urgent as they are, must be constructive and rational. Rioting and violence provide no solutions for economic problems. Much of the justification for rioting has come from the belief that violence has a certain cleansing effect. Perhaps, in a special psychological sense, this is so. But we have seen a better and more constructive cleansing process in our nonviolent demonstrations. Another theory to justify violent revolution is that rioting enables Negroes to overcome their fear of the white man. But they are just as afraid of the power structure after a riot as before. As a matter of fact, I think the spirit of militancy among black militant groups speaks much more of fear than it does of confidence. Ultimately, one's sense of manhood must come from within himself.

Today's dissenters tell the complacent majority that the time has come when further evasion of social responsibility in a turbulent world will invite disaster and death. America has not yet changed because so many think it need not change, but this is the illusion of the damned. America must change because 23,000,000 black citizens will no longer sit back quietly in a wretched past. They have left the valley of despair; they have found strength in struggle; and whether they live or die, they shall never crawl nor retreat again. Joined by their white allies, they will shake the prison walls until they fall. America must change. We will fight for human justice, brotherhood, secure peace, and abundance for all. When we have won these — in a spirit of unshakable nonviolence — then, in luminous splendor, the Christian era will truly begin. (1663 words)

Time:_____

Check It

Write the letter of the correct answer on the line.

___ 1. We cannot take a leisurely approach to the solution of today's problems because
   a) the black man has exploded with fury.
   b) all of the problems are complex and their solutions are urgent.
   c) the nation is not prepared for action to solve those problems.

___ 2. Dr. King feels that the rebellion of the black American is not only inevitable but also

a) undesirable.

b) indefinite.

c) greatly desirable.

___ 3. Schools, transportation, water supply, traffic, and crime

a) would not have been problems without the Negro in our cities.

b) would have been problems whether or not the Negro lived in our cities.

c) are problems quite separate from the problems of the Negro.

___ 4. The election of Negroes to important political offices has shown the Negro that

a) he has the potential to determine his own fate.

b) his opportunities are limited.

c) his vote is really of little importance.

___ 5. Integration of the schools has shown that

a) integration itself solves the problems of inadequacy of the schools.

b) integration itself solves no important problems.

c) integration itself does not solve the problems of inadequacy of the schools.

___ 6. After 1964 the Negro suffered economically because

a) hopeless despair set in.

b) automation cut into jobs badly.

c) housing conditions were worse than ever.

___ 7. The author believes that militancy among black groups

a) speaks more of confidence than it does of fear.

b) speaks more of fear than it does of confidence.

c) will destroy the power structure.

___ 8. America has not yet changed because

a) everyone believes that there must be change.

b) no one really believes that change is necessary.

c) so many people think there is no need for change.

Would You Believe?

You'll remember that in unit 5 you worked with figures of speech, which are expressions that say one thing and mean another thing. They have come down to us through perhaps hundreds of years of communication among people. Below are ten sentences. Find the figure of speech in each and underline it. Then, in the space before each sentence, write a number to show the meaning of the figure of speech. The meanings of the figures of speech are given below.

___ a. Getting that job is really a feather in my cap.

___ b. When he said that, I knew he was really in the groove.

___ c. She swallowed hook, line, and sinker everything Bob said.

___ d. Joe's performance doesn't hold a candle to Richard Burton's.

___ e. When he returned from the war, his family killed the fatted calf.

___ f. Mrs. Blake couldn't resist buying odds and ends at the public sale.

___ g. "Either fish or cut bait," my father said, and I knew that I'd better get my application sent off right away.

___ h. He was a dark horse in the race for governor of the state.

___ i. I don't believe half the scuttlebutt I've heard about Tom.

___ j. When she finished talking, I felt that I'd been taken down a peg or two.

Meanings:

1. Both skill and knowledge were needed when the servant lighted his master's way through the dark streets.

2. When a hunter killed his first bird, he plucked a feather and put it in his cap.

3. The ends of bolts of cloth, none of them matching, were sold at reduced prices.

4. A story in the Bible tells of the welcome of a son, during which the father killed the finest animal for a celebration feast.

5. On sailing ships, this was a cask for water where the men gathered to exchange gossip.

6. To produce good sound, a needle must fit the groove of a record exactly.

7. During days of fishing in small boats, sailors who did not do their work as fishermen were forced to cut up fish to be used as bait.

8. At one time, the flag on a ship was lowered by inserting a bolt or peg in the flagpole.

9. A hungry fish will swallow bait and tackle. A gullible person may believe anything that is told to him.

10. At the racetracks, an unknown horse was seldom expected to win.

Parts Department: Roots

If you know the meaning of a single root, you may understand the meaning of many words. The Latin root *gregis* means a herd or flock. Below are five words that have been formed from that root. Study the word parts carefully and then fit the right word into each of the sentences below.

segregate	*se*, apart + *gregis*, flock + *ate*, act of
congregation	*con*, together + *gregis*, flock + *ion*, result of
aggregate	*ad*, to + *gregis*, flock + *ate*, result of
gregarious	*gregis*, flock + *arious*, having tendency to
egregious	*ex*, out of + *gregis*, flock + *ous*, quality of

1. An attempt was made by the shepherd to _____ the sheep from the goats.

2. He made an _____ blunder, one that turned everyone in the audience against him.

3. Granite is an example of an _____, in which many particles are closely bound together.

4. His _____ nature made him a person who loved to mingle with other people.

5. The minister looked carefully at the members of his _____ before he started to speak.

Well Known

People are always blaming their circumstances for what they are. I don't believe in circumstances. The people who get on in this world are the people who get up and look for the circumstances they want, and, if they can't find them, make them.

GEORGE BERNARD SHAW

Mrs. Warren's Profession, by Bernard Shaw. By permission of The Society of Authors as Agent for the Estate of Bernard Shaw.

Key Words
rebellion–a fight against government; *conflicts*–fights, struggles

---
Absalom

Absalom was the third and favorite son of King David of Israel. Absalom was a handsome and clever young man, but he was jealous of the great power of his father.

Absalom stirred up a rebellion against King David. His followers were no match for the forces of the king. They were defeated, and Absalom fled upon the back of a mule. His head caught in the low-hanging branches of a tree, and he was pulled from the mule. King David had given orders that he should not be harmed. But as he hung there he was slain by Joab, the king's commanding general, and Joab's attendants for the good of the nation.

The story of the grief of King David is told in II Samuel 18. It is one of the most deeply moving passages in the Bible. The tragic story of David and Absalom has been used as a basis for many novels and poems which describe conflicts between a father and his son. The term *Absalom* has come to mean either a favorite son, or a son who rebels against his father. (185 words)

From *The World Book Encyclopedia.* © 1969 Field Enterprises Educational Corporation.

True or False
Mark each statement either true (T) or false (F).

___ 1. Absalom was the favorite son of Joab.

___ 2. Absalom was defeated in a battle against his father's army.

___ 3. Absalom was hanged by command of his father.

___ 4. The story of Absalom is a biblical one.

Parts Department: Dividing Words into Syllables

When a single consonant comes between two vowels, the syllable division is usually made before the consonant, and the first vowel has a long sound. For example: spī/der. Rewrite each word with a line between the syllables. Then mark the first vowel.

1. notice _____ 6. station _____

2. cider _____ 7. lady _____

3. clover _____ 8. music _____

4. believe _____ 9. polar _____

5. nation _____ 10. silence _____

When a single consonant comes between two vowels, the syllable division is sometimes made after the consonant. Then the first vowel has a short sound. For example: fĭn/ish. Rewrite each word with a line between the syllables. Then mark the first vowel.

11. prison _____ 16. cabin _____

12. wagon _____ 17. preface _____

13. lemon _____ 18. second _____

14. liver _____ 19. river _____

15. seven _____ 20. robin _____

When working with an unfamiliar word that has a single consonant between two vowels, divide the word after the first vowel. Say the word, giving the first vowel a long sound. Then, if you do not recognize the word, divide it after the consonant, and give the first vowel a short sound. Rewrite each word with a line between the syllables. Then mark the first vowel.

21. major _____ 24. model _____

22. credit _____ 25. bacon _____

23. dragon _____ 26. feline _____

Key Words
commissioned–gave the power or the duty of doing something;
notorious–well known for something bad

Captain Kidd

William Kidd was a famous Scottish pirate who first worked
as a respectable New York trader and sea captain. In 1695,
King William III of England commissioned him *privateer* (captain of an armed ship) to capture certain notorious pirates
and seize their stolen goods. But he captured no pirates. Instead, he went to Madagascar, where he made friends with
the pirates he had been sent to take. When he later returned
to the West Indies, he learned he had been declared a pirate.
He sailed north and left gold, silver, and Indian goods with
the Gardiner family on Gardiner's Island, N.Y. The English
government seized this treasure, and Kidd was arrested when
he landed at Boston. He was sent to England to be tried for
five acts of piracy and for the murder of his gunner, William
Moore. Kidd was not allowed to have legal advice, and he
could not use his personal papers. He was found guilty and
hanged. Tales and legends quickly grew up about Kidd's sup-
posed buried treasure and bloody deeds. (173 words)

Adapted from *The World Book Encyclopedia.* © 1969 Field Enterprises Educational Corporation.

True or False
Mark each statement either true (T) or false (F).

___ 1. Captain Kidd lived in the 17th century.

___ 2. He had no contact with pirates.

___ 3. Kidd left some treasure with friends in Boston.

___ 4. Kidd was an American.

Parts Department: Dividing Words into Syllables

When two consonants come between two vowels, the syllable division is usually made between the consonants, and the first syllable is usually accented. For example: pas´/ture. Rewrite each word with a line between the syllables. Then place the accent mark on the proper syllable.

1. master _____

2. lumber _____

3. rescue _____

4. obtain _____

5. monkey _____

6. thunder _____

7. lantern _____

8. dismay _____

When the two consonants are alike, the consonant in the accented syllable is sounded, and the consonant in the unaccented syllable is silent. For example: rab´/bit; ap/pear´. Rewrite each word with a line between the syllables. Then place the accent mark on the proper syllable. Cross out the silent consonant.

9. apple _____

10. robber _____

11. valley _____

12. balloon _____

13. dollar _____

14. cabbage _____

15. pepper _____

16. summer _____

An exception to this rule of division may occur when a word has a prefix or suffix. Then the affix is a syllable by itself, and the root is usually accented. For example: dark´/en, de/plane´, gift´/ed. Rewrite each word with a line between the syllables. Then place the accent mark on the proper syllable.

17. stiffer _____

18. inform _____

19. goodness _____

20. jumper _____

21. unlike _____

22. farmer _____

23. replay _____

24. telling _____

Key Words

ballyhoo–noisy advertising; *endowed*–gave money or property; *animate*–to give motion to; *saturated*–filled completely

The Magic Kingdom

His accumulation of 30 Oscars was unequaled in the history of the motion picture industry. He had won 900 other awards and five honorary doctorates (though he never graduated from high school). The corporation bearing his name had grown fourfold in ten years; in 1965 it grossed $110 million—a 27% rise over 1964. The charitable foundation he established without fuss or ballyhoo had generously endowed educational and cultural activities in Southern California. Yet for all of his laurels, Walt Disney was still the busiest man in Hollywood.

...The audience he aimed at was "honest adults." In short, it was himself. "We're selling corn," he said, "and I like corn." ...When Disney decided that the market for animated shorts was becoming saturated, he shifted to nature shorts and then brilliantly original full-length nature features....And when animated features...became impractical, he embarked on live-action "people" films...as well as a variety of smoothly-made TV adventure stories. The Disney approach was visionary to the point of idealism....He refused to deal with unpleasant things....(173 words)

True or False

Mark each statement either true (T) or false (F).

___ 1. All of Disney's films depict the harsh realities of life.

___ 2. Disney had the foresight to change his type of film when the market became saturated with a specific type.

Parts Department: Dividing Words into Syllables

Say these words. Notice where the syllable division occurs in each.

   can•dle   ta•ble   trou•ble   gen•tle   han•dle

Complete this statement: If a word ends in *le* preceded by a _____
_____ that _____ usually begins the last
syllable, and is always pronounced. (Furthermore, this last syllable is
never accented.) This is important to know, because many people, not
pronouncing the consonant before the *le,* will fall into bad pronunciation and spelling habits with these words.

Rewrite these words, dividing them into syllables and placing the
accent mark on the proper syllable.

   sample   _____ turtle   _____

   tremble   _____ ample   _____

   needle   _____ people   _____

The words *buckle* (buk′əl) and *pickle* (pik′əl) are *not* divided into syllables as the above words are. Can you tell, from the phonetic spelling
in the parentheses, why they are not? Look up *jungle* and *single* in your
dictionary. Do they follow the above syllabication rule? Now compare
their pronunciation with *candle.* What pronunciation differences do you
find?

Parts Department: Adding Prefixes and Suffixes to Roots

The Latin root *spirare* means to breathe. There are many words in English which have derived from that root. For instance, the word *spirit*

comes from an early belief that when the breath left the body, it left in the form of the soul.

On this page are some words that have been formed from the root *spirare*. In the spaces following the words, write the prefix and/or suffix for each word. Before the word, identify it with a definition which appears below. Write the number of the definition in the blank before the word. If necessary, use your dictionary.

Definition	Word	Prefix	Root	Suffix
_____	inspire	_____	_____	_____
_____	conspirator	_____	_____	_____
_____	transpire	_____	_____	_____
_____	spirogram	_____	_____	_____
_____	respiration	_____	_____	_____
_____	expire	_____	_____	_____
_____	spiracle	_____	_____	_____
_____	spirometer	_____	_____	_____
_____	perspiration	_____	_____	_____

Definitions:

1. an opening through which air passes during respiration
2. to occur; to happen; to escape, as through the pores
3. one who agrees with (literally, breathes with) another
4. the act of breathing again and again
5. an instrument for measuring the capacity of the lungs
6. to arouse or to produce a feeling
7. to emit the last breath; to die
8. a graph showing the breathing of a person or living thing
9. the act of breathing through the pores, giving off waste materials

Words You Need

Read each sentence and choose the meaning of the word in italics. Write the letter of your answer on the line. Use your dictionary if necessary.

___ 1. When we are young, we don't believe in death; we think we are *immortal*.

Immortal means a) everlasting; b) wicked; c) ghostly.

___ 2. People with *diabetes* must take insulin to stay well.

Diabetes means a) a mental disorder; b) a disability that accompanies old age; c) a disorder of the functioning of the pancreas.

___ 3. The *pancreas* produces substances necessary for digestion.

Pancreas means a) an outgrowth in the stomach due to an injury; b) a gland near the stomach; c) a part of the circulatory system.

___ 4. After playing a hard game of volleyball on an empty stomach, I was *ravenous*.

Ravenous means a) very hungry; b) sickly; c) normal.

___ 5. After days of searching for the buried treasure, we discovered that our map was the wrong one, and the outcome of all our efforts was *nil*.

Nil means a) important; b) unsatisfactory; c) nothing.

___ 6. A thin person with a fast rate of *metabolism* may eat a lot but not gain weight, because his body burns up fuel too fast.

Metabolism means a) process of breathing; b) process of changing in body processes; c) process of moving about.

___ 7. When the pancreas becomes shriveled and *degenerated*, it is unable to send out digestive juices.

Degenerated means a) become invisible; b) become ineffective; c) become smaller in size.

___ 8. After the *filtrate* was strained, many impurities were left behind.

Filtrate means a) a soupy substance; b) substance that has passed through a filter; c) substance that is made from living organs.

___ 9. "This is one of science's greatest discoveries," said the speaker in his *eulogy* to the two doctors.

Eulogy means a) monetary reward; b) silent recognition; c) high praise.

How We Discovered Insulin

Charles H. Best, M.D., as told to J. D. Ratcliff

Dr. Frederick Banting, a medical immortal. The man who came into the laboratory the morning of May 16, 1921, didn't look like a medical immortal. Few do at age 29. Dr. Frederick Banting looked more like a farmer—powerful, with slightly stooped shoulders, blue-green eyes, big nose and jutting stubborn chin. His voice, halting, quiet, betrayed an inborn shyness.

"Let's get started, Mr. Best," he said. "We really haven't much time." What an understatement! He had asked the University of Toronto for the use of a laboratory for eight weeks, for ten dogs, and for the help of someone who knew chemistry and physiology. The money value of his modest request was at most $100. With this he thought he could conquer a disease that had always baffled medical men: the merciless killer, diabetes!

"You read French, don't you?" Banting asked. I did. "Let's go to the library then," he said, "and look up how a Frenchman named Hedon took a pancreas out of a dog."

Diabetes—a disease cursed over 2000 years ago. That was the beginning. We both knew the horror of diabetes—described by a Greek physician 2000 years earlier as "a disease in which the flesh melts away and is siphoned off in the urine." Somehow the bodies of stricken people stopped burning sugar into energy. Instead their bodies turned cannibal, consuming stored fats and proteins. There was always unquenchable thirst—victims often drinking several gallons of water a day while losing a little amount of sugary urine. Their appetite was ravenous. The only treatment was a rigid diet designed to correct the patient's disrupted chemical balance. Severely stricken victims were offered a grim choice: eat well today and die tomorrow, or cut down to a few hundred calories a day and linger for a while in weary befuddlement.

Tragic effects of diabetic attacks. Banting had seen diabetes convert a vivacious 15-year-old girl classmate in Alliston, Ontario, into a pathetic child for whom death came swiftly. At my home in West Pembroke, Maine, I had seen the same happen to my Aunt Anna. A stout, vigorous woman in her early 30's, she wasted to 80 pounds before she died.

The world would have considered us a most unlikely pair to match wits with this killer. I was a 22-year-old graduate student, working for my master's degree in physiology and biochemistry. Banting's experience in research was virtually nil. At his family's urging he had started out to study for the Methodist ministry. But, a halting speaker, he changed to medicine. He had been an average student.

After serving as a surgeon in the Canadian army in World War I, and winning the Military Cross for bravery, he set up practice as an orthopedic surgeon in London, Ontario. He waited for patients who never came. One month his income was four dollars. His fiancee could see little future with such a man, and they parted.

Confident of finding cause of killer disease. Now this man was staking all his meager resources on his hunch that he could cure the sugar sickness. He gave up his little practice, sold his office furniture, books, instruments, everything. Banting couldn't afford another failure.

It was known that the pancreas — a pale-yellow, pollywog-shaped abdominal organ that produces digestive juices — was somehow involved in this disease. In 1889 Oskar Minkowski in Germany had removed a dog's pancreas, mainly to see if the animal could get along without it. Next day he noted flies clustered around puddles of the dog's urine. The urine was sugary; the dog, in normal health the day before, now had diabetes.

Did pancreatic juices, then, contain a factor that normally

regulates the metabolism of sugar? To test the idea, research men tied off the ducts that carry these juices to the intestine. When dogs got this surgery, their pancreases shriveled and degenerated—but they did not get diabetes! The shriveled organs, unable to send digestive secretions to the intestines, were still producing the anti-diabetic factor.

Long, weary months of research. But, if it wasn't in the pancreatic juices, where was it? Attention shifted to the thousands of mysterious little "islet" cells scattered through the pancreas and surrounded by tiny capillaries. Did they secrete some "X" stuff, perhaps a hormone that regulated the burning of sugar? And did they empty it, then, not into the intestine but into the bloodstream? Several research men had suggested as much and had gone hunting for the elusive hormone. But all had come home with empty game bags.

Now, it was our turn. "Maybe it's this way, Mr. Best," Banting said—not for several days would we be Fred and Charley. "Maybe when the researchers remove a healthy pancreas and grind it up to extract this X stuff, enzymes in the digestive juice mix with the X stuff and destroy it—just as they break down proteins in the intestine. Maybe that's why no one has been able to find it."

Knowing that when the pancreatic ducts are tied off, the cells which secrete digestive juices degenerate faster than do the islet cells, we would tie off these ducts in dogs and wait. "In seven to ten weeks the pancreas will degenerate, stop making digestive juice—and there will be nothing to destroy the X stuff. You extract it. Then we'll give this extract to a diabetic dog and see if it lowers the sugar in blood and urine."

I did my chemical work in our cubbyhole lab. Dog surgery was performed two flights up in the skylighted attic. Before summer was over, that attic became as steamy as any Turkish bath. To get some relief we wore little or nothing under our white lab coats. Since money was short, we ate in the lab. Eggs and sausage fried over a Bunsen burner became diet staples.

One serious problem was a scarcity of dogs. When the situation became acute, Banting said, "Crank up The Pancreas,

Charley, and let's go." (This was our name for his Model T Ford.) We rattled through the poorer parts of Toronto, hunting for dogs whose owners would part with them for a dollar.

We had tied off the first pancreatic ducts in May, and in early July we expected the pancreases to be shriveled, the X stuff accessible. We opened one of the animals and found the pancreas blooming with health, no atrophy, no shriveling. Banting and I had tied the ducts incorrectly.

Our eight weeks were almost up. This would have been as good a time as any to accept defeat. But Banting was a stubborn man. During the war he had gotten an ugly shrapnel wound in his right arm. Doctors had wanted to amputate. Banting refused—and nursed the arm back to health. Now we were going to nurse our sickly project back to health.

Prof. John J. R. Macleod, head of the physiology department, who had provided us with work facilities, was on vacation in Europe. "He won't know the difference if we stay on," we decided. We began re-operating on the dogs, tying off ducts, correctly this time. On July 27, we got the beautifully shriveled, degenerated pancreas we wanted. It should contain the X stuff—if the X stuff existed.

Now we sliced and froze the mixture. We allowed it to thaw slowly, ground it up and filtered it through paper. A dying diabetic dog was waiting, too weak to lift his head. Fred injected 5 c.c. of the filtrate into a vein. The dog *looked* a little better—but self-delusion is easy at such times. Blood tests were needed.

Success in experimentation with dogs. I drew a few droplets from the dog's paw and began testing for blood sugar. Banting hovered over me. If sugar were heavily present, the reagent in the test tube would turn deep red; little sugar and it would be a pale pink. There was a new test every hour and the reagent was getting paler, paler. Blood sugar was going down—from 0.20 percent, to 0.12 percent to....It was headed for a normal 0.09 percent! This was the most exciting moment of Banting's life or my own.

Life now became a blurred nightmare of work. This thing had to be nailed down. Dogs had to be injected, blood had to be drawn for testing, urine collected. It was an hourly, round-the-clock schedule. We stretched out on lab benches to get what sleep we could.

But there was an ever-reviving miracle for us to behold: dogs glassy-eyed with the sleep of death upon them; then, a few hours later, they were up, eating, tails wagging. Jolted back to life, one dog lived 12 days, another 22 days. Our pet was Marjorie—dog number 33. Black and white, vaguely collie, she learned to jump up on a bench, hold out her paw to give us a blood sample and keep still to get the shot on which her life depended. For 70 days she was alive, well. Then we ran out of the extract, isletin, as we then called it. (Only later did Macleod persuade us to change the name to insulin.)

It took almost all the isletin we could extract from a degenerated pancreas to keep one dog alive for one day. How far would this go toward keeping alive millions of diabetics around the world?

Slaughterhouse to the rescue. Fred remembered reading that the pancreas of an unborn animal was mainly islet cells —since the digestive juice wasn't needed in the womb. As a farm boy, he also knew that farmers frequently bred cows before sending them to the slaughterhouse to hoist weight. Wouldn't pancreases from the unborn calves be rich in isletin? We cranked up The Pancreas and headed for a slaughterhouse. Later, back at the lab, we ground up the salvaged pancreases, extracted, purified, and reaped a rich harvest of isletin.

We could now keep dogs alive as long as we wanted. Eventually, of course, it was found that with improved extraction methods any animal pancreas—sheep, hog, cow—provided insulin. There was going to be enough for all needs.

By November 14 we were ready to share some of our excitement with the world. Before the Journal Club of the Department of Physiology, Banting and I gave our first paper —complete with lantern slides showing blood-sugar charts. But the crucial question still had to be answered. *Would insulin work in human beings?*

Across the street in Toronto General Hospital was 14-year-old Leonard Thompson. After two years with diabetes, he was down to 65 pounds, had scarcely the strength to lift his head from the pillow. By the usual criteria he would have, at most, only a few weeks left.

We had established that an insulin "cocktail," taken by mouth, did not work. So now Banting and I rolled up our sleeves. I injected him with our extract and he injected me — we had to be sure it wasn't too toxic to be tolerated by human beings. Next day we had slightly sore arms, that was all.

Experimentation on humans. So in January, 1922, the wasted little arm of the dying boy was injected. Testing began. All over again, it was the story of our dogs. Blood sugar dropped — dramatically. Leonard began to eat normal meals. Sunken cheeks filled out, new life came to weary muscles. Leonard was going to live! (He lived another 13 years and died in 1935 — of pneumonia following a motorcycle accident.) He was the first of dozens, then hundreds, thousands, millions to get insulin.

Success at last! Honors began to shower on us. For the best piece of research conducted at the university that year we were awarded the Reeve Prize — a welcome $50. A grateful Parliament voted Banting a life annuity of $7500. Then came a great research institute for him, and later one named for me. When Banting won the Nobel Prize in 1923, he shared the money equally with me.

Both of us stayed on at the university, and through the succeeding years concentrated on our individual research projects. But the excitement of the old days was missing. Then on a wintry February day in 1941, we were walking across the campus. "Charley," said Banting, "let's start working together again. You handle the chemistry, and I'll..."

It was not to be. Three days later Banting — now Major Sir Frederick Banting, working on problems of aviation medicine — was aboard a two-engine bomber bound for England. The plane crashed in a snowstorm in a forest near Musgrave Harbor, Newfoundland. Banting, with a lung punctured by crushed ribs, used his waning strength to bandage the wounds of the pilot, the only survivor. Then he lay down on pine boughs in the snow and went into the sleep from which he would never waken.

Of all eulogies, perhaps most moving was the one spoken five years later at a London gathering of the Diabetics Association: "Without Banting this meeting could have been only a gathering of ghosts bemoaning their fate." (2144 words)

Time:_____

Check It

Write the letter of the answer on the line.

___ 1. How would you describe Dr. Frederick Banting?

a) A slightly built, quiet individual.

b) A powerfully built man with a strong, booming voice.

c) A husky man with a quiet voice and shy personality.

___ 2. Who is telling this story of Dr. Banting?

a) One of Dr. Banting's students.

b) A historian.

c) A partner in Dr. Banting's experiments and discovery.

___ 3. Why were these medical scientists interested in finding a cure for diabetes?

a) Diabetes was a relatively new disease.

b) There was a reward for the discovery of a cure.

c) Both men had seen diabetes end the lives of some people close to them.

___ 4. What were some of the physical symptoms of diabetes?

a) Unquenchable thirst and hunger.

b) Desire for prolonged sleep.

c) Sleeplessness.

___ 5. What abdominal organ was involved in the disease?

a) Liver.

b) Pancreas.

c) Heart.

____ 6. What one factor do you think helped the doctors to achieve their goal in saving diabetic patients?
   a) Desire for reward and fame.
   b) Desire to continue research.
   c) Unwillingness to accept defeat.

Sound Sense: Consonant Review

Mark the consonants in these words. Underline all blends; circle all digraphs; and draw a diagonal line through all silent consonants. For example: although.

1. spring
2. ludicrous
3. chaos
4. scenic
5. budget

6. atmosphere
7. principal
8. pneumonia
9. astronauts
10. alphabet

11. chamois
12. allotted
13. shower
14. prescribe
15. structure

Sound Sense: Vowel Review

Mark all vowels in these words. Put this mark ‾ over vowels that have a long sound; put this mark ˇ over vowels that have a short sound; put this mark / through vowels that are silent; put this symbol ə over vowels that have a schwa sound; and underline diphthongs.

1. replay
2. contradict
3. recognize
4. hoisted
5. growth

6. scout
7. collide
8. yellow
9. pleasant
10. abrim

11. though
12. drone
13. allow
14. central
15. flamboyant

Alliteration and Onomatopoeia

Alliteration is the repetition of the same first sound in a group of words or line of poetry. In "Peter Piper picked a peck of pickled peppers," the "p" sounds are examples of alliteration.

Onomatopoeia is the formation of a name or word by imitating the sound associated with the thing designated. Examples: the *buzzing* of a bee; the *hoot* of an owl; the *fizz* of soda water.

In each of the following sentences write whether alliteration or onomatopoeia is used:

1. The low growl of the bear gave me a feeling of uneasiness.

_____

2. The slippery stump of the salamander's tail seemed to be very sensitive.

_____

3. The gurgling, babbling brook gave sound like lively laughter.

_____

4. The hippos wallowed in the oozing mud while they enjoyed themselves in the sun.

_____

Write your own examples of alliteration and onomatopoeia.

5. _____

6. _____

7. _____

8. _____

9. _____

10. _____

11. _____

12. _____

13. _____

14. _____

15. _____

Words You Need

Read each sentence and choose the meaning of the word in italics. Write the letter of your answer on the line. Use your dictionary if necessary.

— 1. The returning astronauts were faced with a *barrage* of questions from the reporters.
   Barrage means: a) number; b) heavy attack; c) variety.

— 2. The *barricade* in the road was built with trees and stones.
   Barricade means: a) obstruction; b) trench; c) line.

— 3. Differences in *environment* often account for differences in the way plants and animals develop.
   Environment means: a) structure; b) form; c) surroundings.

— 4. His *prowess* as a top pitcher was feared by batters throughout the league.
   Prowess means: a) success; b) bravery; c) skill.

— 5. We were *deterred* from entering the house by a big dog that growled as we approached.
   Deterred means: a) frightened; b) prevented; c) aided.

— 6. Even though Julie gave up easily, Amy had the *tenacity* to stay until the end of the contest.
   Tenacity means: a) tenderness; b) money; c) firmness.

All the Way Up

In the dressing room of the elegant Wimbledon clubhouse two American girls practiced curtsies. Neither one was particularly adept at the task, but they were deadly serious about it. Then it was time for the match. Darlene Hard and Althea Gibson stepped onto the tennis court, faced the royal box, and curtsied to the Queen of England. The crowd roared a welcome as each girl swung lightly to her side of the court.

This was the final match—the one that would determine the winner of the highly-prized Wimbledon Cup of 1957. And Althea Gibson, the long-legged, light-footed girl from the slums of New York City, wanted to win that cup more than she had ever wanted anything in her whole life.

At the umpire's signal, the match began. The cheers of the tennis-wise crowd echoed each well-played point of the closely matched girls. When finally Althea smashed home that winning point, she ran to the net and shook hands with her opponent. Then both girls turned toward the trophy table. A red carpet had been rolled out from the royal box to the trophy table, and the Queen, looking cool and beautiful in the hot sunshine, advanced down the carpet. For a moment, Althea hesitated; then she curtsied deeply to the Queen and shook the hand that had been extended to her. She clutched her gold tray, curtsied again, and turned to face a barrage of reporters and photographers.

For just a moment, it occurred to Althea that all of this had to be a fairy tale. How could a wild, skinny tomboy from the dirty, overcrowded streets of Harlem—miles from a tennis court—learn to play tennis well enough to capture the Wimbledon Cup? How could anyone change worlds in the space of a few short years? How did a girl who was a street-fighting school dropout such a short while ago become a gracious college-educated woman who was the toast of nations for her prowess on the tennis courts?

Althea could tell you that she had come a long way from that farm in South Carolina where she was born in 1927. The move with the family to a small apartment in Harlem, the Negro district of New York City, had occurred when Althea was only three. She grew up on the streets, and she was one of the wildest competitors in any game. School was a sheer waste of time, when she could be shooting baskets in the park, collecting empty bottles to cash in for a few pennies, or sneaking into the movies.

A child had to learn to take care of herself on the streets of Harlem, and Althea's father taught her to fight with her fists. There are a few people around today who can testify that Althea learned her lessons well. But, she was rapidly becoming a product of her environment—tough, wild, uneducated.

It was paddle tennis that really gave her direction. When the streets of Harlem were closed with wooden barricades so the children could play, Althea was on the paddle tennis court. And when she was only 12 years old, she won the New York City championship.

When Buddy Walker discovered her, he knew he had a job on his hands if he was going to discipline Althea for competition on the tennis courts. Althea had dropped out of school at the end of the seventh grade. Counter girl in a nut shop, elevator operator in a hotel, packer in a button factory, chicken cleaner in a meat market—those were some of the jobs she held and lost because she was not always dependable. Nevertheless, Buddy bought her the first tennis racket she ever held, and made it possible for her to practice on the Harlem River Courts. It wasn't long before Walker and a lot of other people knew that they had a winner on their hands, if they could only teach Althea to control her temper.

The New York State Open Championship in 1942 was a turning point in her life. She won that tournament easily, and there was no doubt that she could go further. Then she attracted the attention of two people who were to make a great difference in her life: the two doctors, Hubert Easton and Robert Johnson. To the Easton home in Wilmington, North Carolina, Althea went in 1946. There she finished her high school work and learned something about refined family life. It wasn't easy, because she still preferred hanging out in the pool halls. But, Dr. Easton and Dr. Johnson were teaching her to play tennis, and that was enough to keep her struggling.

Three years of high school were followed by a scholarship to Florida A & M, the Negro college at Tallahassee. She earned forty dollars a month by cleaning the equipment in the gym. In 1950, she was invited to play in the national tournament at Forest Hills. She lost to Louise Brough, but she had come very close to victory.

In 1955 the State Department asked Althea to tour Southeast Asia with three other tennis players in order to build good will towards America. Then came the chance to compete at Wimbledon and final success. When she returned to New York from England, Mayor Wagner of New York gave a luncheon in her honor. Then the little girl from the streets of Harlem was treated to a ticker-tape parade down Fifth Avenue. Later, when she won the championship at Forest Hills, Althea knew that her wildest dreams had been realized.

A modern-day Cinderella? Hardly. Nothing came to Althea Gibson by magic. She was poor, a Negro, a child of the slums, but nothing had deterred her from becoming one of the greatest tennis players of all time. And while she was at it, she'd also become a well-educated, charming person as well as a symbol of tenacity. Once she had a grip on a better life, she didn't let go. (991 words)

Time:_____

True or False

Mark each statement either true (T) or false (F).

___ 1. Althea Gibson won the tournament at Forest Hills the first time she competed.

___ 2. The story of Miss Gibson illustrates that you really can't overcome the influences of environment.

___ 3. Despite her background, Althea was always a person who wanted a good education.

___ 4. Althea was frequently not dependable on the jobs that she held.

___ 5. Althea earned some of her expenses at Florida A & M.

___ 6. Althea Gibson is an example of a person who made it to the top entirely alone.

___ 7. The Wimbledon Cup tournament was held at Forest Hills.

___ 8. Learning to control her temper and to act with graciousness was not easy for Althea.

___ 9. Althea was discovered by Dr. Easton, who bought her the first tennis racket that she ever owned.

___10. The author implies that getting to the top in anything is easy if one simply has the desire to win.

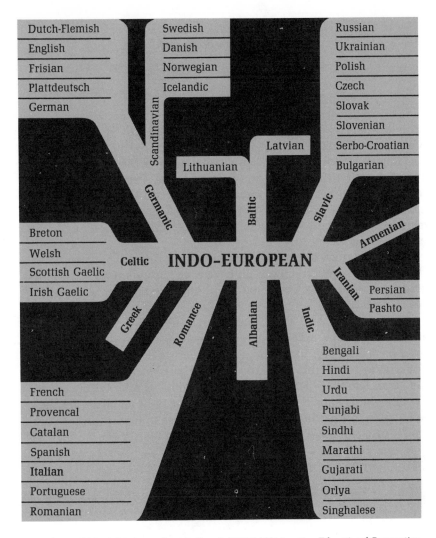

Dutch-Flemish	Swedish	Russian
English	Danish	Ukrainian
Frisian	Norwegian	Polish
Plattdeutsch	Icelandic	Czech
German		Slovak
		Slovenian
	Latvian	Serbo-Croatian
	Lithuanian	Bulgarian

Scandinavian

Germanic Baltic Slavic Armenian

Breton
Welsh Celtic **INDO-EUROPEAN**
Scottish Gaelic Iranian
Irish Gaelic Persian
Pashto

Greek Romance Albanian Indic

Bengali
Hindi
French Urdu
Provencal Punjabi
Catalan Sindhi
Spanish Marathi
Italian Gujarati
Portuguese Orlya
Romanian Singhalese

From *The World Book Dictionary* front matter. © 1969 Field Enterprises Educational Corporation.

Half of the people in the world speak a language that comes from the largest language family, Indo-European. Notice that there are ten branches of this family, and that except for the Armenian, Greek, and Albanian branches, each branch has spread into at least two other languages. Which branch shows the most languages? Did the language that your family speaks or has spoken come from one of the Indo-European languages?

Direction or Confusion?

It's a well-known fact that most people lack skills in taking and giving clear directions. How many times during the day do you say, "Repeat that for me," or "How's that again?" Most people don't pay careful attention during the first stages of directions that they receive from someone else; apparently they do this because they know they can always say, "Say that again, please." Think of the wasted time for both the person who asks for directions and the person who is asked to give directions!

Oral directions appear to be particularly difficult for people to follow. Below are directions given by an attendant in a service station. Read the directions once. Without looking back, attempt to draw a simple map.

"Quimby, you say? Why, that's only a few miles from here. Go east from here one mile to the crossroads. You'll see a red schoolhouse on the far left-hand corner. Turn left there and continue for ¾ of a mile to another crossroads. Continue north for another ½ mile. Turn left there for a quarter of a mile and take the first turn to your right. Go north again a mile. On your right you'll see a small road angling off to the far right. Take that and follow it through the woods for a mile and a half. You're in Quimby."

The Library Card Catalog

Learning to use the library is an important skill for success in school. The following questions point out important information about the use of a card catalog. Be sure to go to the library if you need to, to find the answers to these questions.

1. Where is the card catalog in your library?

2: Why is the card catalog important?

3. How is a card catalog like the index of a book?

4. Why are the entries in a card catalog printed on cards?

5. What does the label on the outside of the tray tell you?

_____

_____

_____

6. There are three types of cards in the card catalog. Name them.

_____

_____

_____

7. What information can be found on a typical card in the card catalog?

_____

_____

_____

_____

8. What is the purpose of the call number?

_____

_____

_____

9. What do the numbers in the call number represent?

_____

_____

_____

10. In what order are the parts of the author's name printed on an author card? _____

11. How do subject cards differ from author and title cards in format?

_____

_____

_____

_____

12. Describe the purpose of a cross-reference card. _____

_____

_____

_____

13. How do guide cards help? _____

_____

_____

_____

14. Why do you often find temporary cards in your library's card catalog? (They will often be on a different kind of paper than the regular cards.)

_____

_____

_____

15. How would a title card be filed alphabetically if the first word were a number? _____

_____

_____

16. A book with the title *The New America* would be filed alphabetically under what letter? _____

_____

_____

17. What would be some time-saving hints on the use of the card catalog? _____

_____

_____

_____

18. One important source of information you must not neglect is the librarian. When should you ask for help? _____

_____

_____

_____

_____

_____

_____

Skills Review

Prefixes of Number. Fill in the blanks to complete these sentences.

1. A_____ syllabic word has three syllables.

2. It is said that a _____ pede has a hundred feet.

3. In music an octave consists of _____ tones.

4. Monoxide has _____ atom of oxygen in each molecule.

5. _____ focals are glasses with two different focal lengths.

Sounds of C and G. Write S above each *c* and *g* that has a soft sound; write H above each *c* and *g* that has a hard sound.

1. cigarette	5. acetate	9. gym	13. coerce
2. succession	6. gyroscope	10. gainful	14. gem
3. celery	7. cogent	11. cyclops	15. gander
4. suggested	8. gigantic	12. crypt	16. succinct

Sounds of W and Y. Write C above each *w* and *y* that has a consonant sound; write V above each *w* and *y* that has a vowel sound.

1. willowy	5. trawler	9. synonym	13. annoy
2. brawl	6. hygiene	10. witty	14. wayward
3. woodwork	7. symbol	11. wispy	15. yeast
4. towel	8. yearly	12. yawn	16. apply

Syllabication. Use diagonal lines to divide these words into syllables.

1. strawberry	4. whatever	7. suppose	10. geometry
2. chicken	5. September	8. location	11. accent
3. gentlemen	6. machine	9. bracelet	12. principle

Accents. Place accent marks on the proper syllables.

1. in fec tion
2. hos pi tal
3. cy press
4. de ter mine
5. chim ney
6. co ag u late
7. hor ri ble
8. a tom ic
9. king dom
10. peo ple
11. re port
12. dis tance

Syllabication and Accents. Divide these words into syllables and place the accent marks where they belong.

1. butterfly
2. syllable
3. season
4. success
5. influence
6. rebelling
7. complex
8. social
9. violence
10. current
11. poetry
12. reasoning

Phonetic Spelling. Write the correct spelling for each of the words spelled phonetically.

1. īz _____
2. ə lōn´ _____
3. nā´chər _____
4. īs _____
5. pīz _____
6. sins _____
7. hī´wā _____
8. skrēm _____

Appendix

Basic Skills Survey

Read the directions carefully for each part of this survey. Record your answers in the spaces provided.

Part I: Sound Sense

A. Underline the word on the right that has the same sound as illustrated on the left.

1. <u>i</u> as in m<u>i</u>crophone   initial   military   flit   nylon

2. <u>ch</u> as in <u>ch</u>orus   chair   machine   cope   chimney

3. <u>th</u> as in ba<u>the</u>   think   both   these   thumb

4. <u>oo</u> as in sp<u>oo</u>n   stood   baboon   shook   took

5. <u>ou</u> as in <u>ou</u>ch   shout   touch   sought   though

6. <u>s</u> as in <u>s</u>ugar   raisin   sound   shade   treasure

7. <u>c</u> as in i<u>c</u>e   cast   lack   racial   sign

8. <u>s</u> as in wa<u>s</u>   sure   leisure   sand   zip

9. <u>al</u> as in w<u>al</u>k   alike   caught   gallon   talcum

10. <u>g</u> as in <u>g</u>eneral   gout   ghost   jewel   great

11. <u>y</u> as in m<u>y</u>   bike   away   funny   yet

12. <u>a</u> as in <u>a</u>mong   alto   lesson   ideal   mate

B. Circle all blends, underline all digraphs, and draw diagonal lines through all silent consonants in these words.

1. paragraph   4. graphics   7. programmed   10. thoughtful

2. blunt   5. grammar   8. height   11. thumbprint

3. whistle   6. diploma   9. impeach   12. philosophy

C. Over each s write an S if it has the sound of sit, write Z if it has the sound of his, write SH if it has the sound of sugar, and write ZH if it has the sound of pleasure.

1. ourselves   4. mission   7. measure   10. distrust

2. sugary   5. phrases   8. insurance   11. surprise

3. reason   6. resistance   9. pension   12. persons

D. Write S above each c and g that has a soft sound; write H above each c and g that has a hard sound.

1. success   4. cyclometer   7. congenial   10. cascade

2. suggest   5. collegian   8. danger   11. gesture

3. conducive   6. practice   9. cyanide   12. fragile

E. Write C above each w and y that has a consonant sound; write V above each w and y that has a vowel sound.

1. willowy   3. magnify   5. pewter   7. bowl   9. reward

2. weary   4. yeoman   6. vying   8. reply   10. borrow

Part II: Parts Department

A. Add -*ing* to the words in the first column, -*able* to the words in the middle column, and -*ous* to the words in the last column. Be sure to make changes in spelling wherever necessary.

1. amuse _____   4. admire _____   7. fame _____

2. scrap _____   5. remark _____   8. glamor _____

3. benefit _____   6. service _____   9. courage _____

B. Complete each compound word by adding one of these words: *stain, power, out, cast, land, piece, stake, hand, work, spread.*

1. sweep _____   4. mouth _____   7. blood _____

2. wide _____   5. wash _____   8. horse _____

3. back _____   6. father _____   9. net _____

C. Write the number of syllables you hear in each of these words.

1. computer _____ 3. pentagon _____ 5. degree _____ 7. area _____

2. pollution _____ 4. telephone _____ 6. bigamy _____ 8. chaotic _____

D. Rewrite each word with a line between the syllables. Then mark the accented syllables.

1. changeable _____   5. president _____

2. percentage _____   6. argument _____

3. unrelated _____   7. official _____

4. discussion _____   8. hospitality _____

E. Underline the prefix in each word and write the meaning of the prefix in the space provided.

1. discontented _____
2. unpleased _____
3. inability _____
4. impossible _____
5. irreplaceable _____
6. illogical _____
7. relive _____
8. precede _____
9. exclude _____
10. miscast _____

11. permit _____
12. recall _____
13. exhale _____
14. polygon _____
15. monotone _____
16. centigrade _____
17. bicycle _____
18. decade _____
19. tripod _____
20. unicorn _____

F. Each of these words contains a suffix. Write the suffix in the space provided.

1. typist _____
2. biology _____
3. cloudy _____
4. excitement _____
5. resistance _____
6. graduation _____
7. collector _____

8. burdensome _____
9. wooden _____
10. cheerful _____
11. fiendish _____
12. forcible _____
13. president _____
14. energetic _____

G. Each of these words contains a common root from Greek or Latin. Underline the root and write its meaning in the space provided.

1. phonics _____
2. psychotic _____
3. bigamy _____
4. monochrome _____
5. geology _____
6. diameter _____
7. pesticide _____

8. periscope _____
9. manacle _____
10. hydroid _____
11. automatic _____
12. report _____
13. congregation _____
14. aspire _____

226

name _____class _____ date _____

H. Place each word part in the appropriate column.

	Prefix	Root	Suffix
1. submission	_____	_____	_____
2. committed	_____	_____	_____
3. remittance	_____	_____	_____
4. permissible	_____	_____	_____
5. mission	_____	_____	_____
6. transmitter	_____	_____	_____
7. emit	_____	_____	_____
8. missile	_____	_____	_____
9. admit	_____	_____	_____
10. dismissed	_____	_____	_____
11. emissary	_____	_____	_____
12. intermittent	_____	_____	_____
13. remiss	_____	_____	_____
14. missionary	_____	_____	_____

Test Yourself: Vowels

A. Underline all words that contain vowels having a long sound.

1. improve	5. either	9. miser	13. system	17. reach
2. phrases	6. extend	10. match	14. science	18. music
3. critical	7. nature	11. provide	15. useful	19. estate
4. open	8. profit	12. seize	16. adult	20. royal

B. Underline all words that contain vowels having a short sound.

1. credit	5. choice	9. gyrate	13. awake	17. tunnel
2. grade	6. stock	10. tennis	14. connect	18. apply
3. theft	7. scissors	11. formula	15. written	19. invest
4. vacate	8. ambush	12. tripped	16. octopus	20. broom

C. Underline each word that contains a schwa sound.

1. happy	5. around	9. invalid	13. America	17. equip
2. slogan	6. idea	10. minus	14. concern	18. material
3. consume	7. infect	11. across	15. guide	19. staff
4. plain	8. output	12. calcium	16. arena	20. race

D. Identify the vowel sounds in the following words. Put ⁻ over each long vowel; put ˇ over each short vowel; put ə over each *schwa* sound; put / through each silent vowel.

1. stream	5. irritate	9. resist	13. boldest	17. plays
2. pygmy	6. phrase	10. reason	14. poetic	18. confuse
3. oppose	7. denial	11. unbind	15. guise	19. beneath
4. golden	8. locket	12. fungus	16. guinea	20. agree

E. The first word in each line has a vowel that is underlined. Underline the word containing the same vowel sound.

1. final:	native	piece	guide	4. shack: flavor flat among
2. lemon:	echo	move	arise	5. beam: reason shell great
3. cute:	stunt	fuel	route	6. ago: chant comma radio

7. gem: view   dent   break   10. split: isle   list   bind

8. sold: blot   clock   comb   11. bunk: tube   until   churn

9. April: pact   weigh   batch   12. blind: mill   deny   winter

F. Underline the word that means the same as the first word.

1. feather: plum   plume   6. whirling: spining   spinning

2. ill will: spite   spit   7. spilled: slopped   sloped

3. slender: slime   slim   8. prong: tine   tin

4. location: site   sit   9. penalty: fin   fine

5. to smooth: plan   plane   10. thorn: spin   spine

G. Before each word write L if the word has a long vowel sound; write S
if the word has a short vowel sound; write N if the vowel sound is
neither long nor short.

_____ 1. stream   _____ 9. extend   _____17. create

_____ 2. passive   _____10. rotate   _____18. squeak

_____ 3. salmon   _____11. firm   _____19. quails

_____ 4. gauge   _____12. charm   _____20. expense

_____ 5. yearn   _____13. poach   _____21. purse

_____ 6. dunce   _____14. maize   _____22. retake

_____ 7. light   _____15. curse   _____23. ledge

_____ 8. retail   _____16. people   _____24. crowd

H. Circle the words in which *ow* or *ou* have the sound of *cow* or *house;*
underline the words in which *oi* or *oy* have the sound of *boil* or *boy.*

1. thought   6. cloister   11. chowder   16. powder   21. pouch

2. crowd   7. prow   12. devour   17. brought   22. pronounce

3. voucher   8. quoit   13. typhoid   18. blown   23. corduroy

4. hoist   9. through   14. royalty   19. throw   24. destroyer

5. blouse   10. moisten   15. slow   20. avoid   25. ought

name _____ class _____ date _____

I.   Underline the words that have the sound of ô as in *talk, author,* and *raw.*

1. hawk   5. drawn   9. walk   13. mallet   17. awkward

2. fall   6. salmon   10. awful   14. pale   18. although

3. taught   7. ballet   11. balance   15. gall   19. aware

4. alike   8. faucet   12. ally   16. taught   20. augment

J.   Add *or, ur, ir, er,* or *ar* to each word to complete its spelling.

1. Gramm___ gives me a lot of trouble.

2. There are many iceb___gs in Arctic waters.

3. Mary is such a fl___t!

4. Jim will surely become a sail___ .

5. The auto suddenly b___st into flames.

6. We had pie a la mode for dess___t.

7. Jim brought my little brother a t___tle.

8. Her short sk___t caused a sensation.

9. My sister has always wanted to become a n___se.

10. Rod is famous for his fast c___ve balls.

11. Remember to keep a f___m grip on your club.

12. Lotus plants thrive in dark, m___ky waters.

K.   Pronounce each word carefully. Then write in the proper column the sound that each vowel stands for. The first one has been done for you.

Word	Short	Long	Diphthong	Schwa	Silent
1. contain		*a*		*o*	*i*
2. beach					
3. sedative					
4. sailfish					

5. enjoy   _____

6. pronounce   _____

7. diabetic   _____

8. thyroid   _____

9. health   _____

10. awesome   _____

11. giant   _____

12. accident   _____

13. contingent   _____

14. growing   _____

15. profound   _____

Test Yourself: Consonants

A. Underline the consonant blends in these words.

1. obstacles
5. indiscriminate
9. sleekness
13. nutrition

2. bespectacled
6. depressant
10. plea
14. gracious

3. fraud
7. break
11. scorn
15. extremist

4. flagrant
8. exploit
12. construct
16. secrete

B. Draw a diagonal line through the silent consonant in these words.

1. psyche
6. knuckle
11. islet
16. pneumonia
21. sleigh

2. through
7. nestle
12. terrain
17. diarrhea
22. stallion

3. ghetto
8. glisten
13. rallies
18. knowledge
23. wrought

4. gnash
9. sullen
14. knew
19. pseudonym
24. science

5. bough
10. height
15. knight
20. rhubarb
25. acknowledge

C. Underline the consonant digraphs in these words.

1. whether
6. athletic
11. challenge
16. cacophony
21. worthwhile

2. myth
7. diminish
12. thrombosis
17. quench
22. flinch

3. atrophy
8. changeable
13. sheltered
18. enough
23. enchantment

4. hunch
9. ethical
14. whither
19. flashlight
24. wreathe

5. phrase
10. thermal
15. champion
20. euphony
25. chimney

D. Write Z over the s if it sounds like *his;* write S if it sounds like *sit;*
write SH if it sounds like *sugar;* write ZH if it sounds like *treasure.*

1. reprisal
4. lose
7. measure
10. mason
13. surprise

2. expansive
5. pleasure
8. absolve
11. raisin
14. because

3. visionary
6. misnomer
9. chiseler
12. surely
15. sugary

E. Write S above each *c* and *g* that has a soft sound; write H above each *c* and *g* that has a hard sound.

1. congenial
2. geography
3. succeed
4. tolerance
5. consequence
6. decadence
7. ginger
8. acoustics
9. merge
10. suggest
11. epidemic
12. circus
13. concentrate
14. glaucoma
15. refugee
16. recipient
17. concrete
18. hallucinogen
19. citation
20. gigantic
21. bicycle
22. pneumococci
23. gymnasium
24. warmonger
25. regurgitate
26. science
27. circumnavigate
28. concentric

F. Write C above each *y* that has a consonant sound; write V above each *y* that has a vowel sound.

1. lymph
2. rye
3. Pyrex
4. oyster
5. lawyer
6. laundry
7. thyroid
8. system
9. play
10. hymn
11. deny
12. crying
13. yucca
14. pyramid
15. yield
16. cynical
17. history
18. yacht
19. yesteryear
20. yellowy
21. psychotic
22. tricycle
23. yummy
24. xylophone
25. pussyfoot
26. python
27. midyear
28. yearly
29. rusty
30. youth

G. Write C above each *w* that is a consonant; write V above each *w* that is a vowel.

1. warranty
2. bellow
3. awaken
4. awful
5. blew
6. browsing
7. aweigh
8. award
9. shallow
10. weariness
11. homeward
12. washwoman
13. whale
14. crown
15. withdraw
16. whitewash
17. Wordsworth
18. screw
19. wrestle
20. brown
21. blown
22. wriggle
23. wageworker
24. Warsaw
25. watchtower
26. ownership
27. withdrawn
28. allowance
29. yawn
30. awhile
31. Newton
32. wristwatch
33. follow
34. waste
35. whistle

H. Pronounce each word carefully. Then write each consonant or consonant combination in the proper column. The first one has been done for you.

Word	Voiced Consonants	Consonant Blend	Digraph	Silent
1. although	*l*		*th*	*gh*
2. bellow				
3. perish				
4. thermal				
5. philosophy				
6. completely				
7. immersed				
8. rhetorical				
9. massive				
10. suggest				
11. degrees				
12. propagandist				
13. shrouded				
14. pneumococcus				
15. orthocephalic				

Test Yourself: Adding Endings—Vowel and Consonant

A. Complete the following statements.

1. When a word ends in a final e, the e is usually dropped when adding a _____ ending. (Example: admirable)

2. However, when words ending in ce and ge are followed by vowel endings beginning with ____ or ____ , the final e is not dropped. (Examples: noticeable, courageous)

3. When a _____ ending is added to a word ending in a final e, no change is made in the root word. (Example: lovely)

4. When a word or accented syllable ends in a single consonant preceded by a single vowel, that consonant is doubled when adding _____ endings. (Example: beginning)

B. Rewrite the following words with their endings. Then write the number of the above statement that applies to the spelling. The first one has been done for you.

1. care + less   *careless — 3*

2. leisure + ly _____

3. concur + ence _____

4. sale + able _____

5. commit + al _____

6. advance + ment _____

7. charge + able _____

8. shine + y _____

9. ship + ed _____

10. change + able _____

11. benefit + ing _____

12. ice + y _____

13. continue + ance _____

14. beg + ing _____

15. marriage + able _____

16. tap + ed _____

C. Rewrite the following words with their endings.

1. thank + ful _____
2. judge + ing _____
3. prefer + ing _____
4. guide + ance _____
5. knowledge + able _____
6. gallop + ing _____
7. indirect + ly _____
8. believe + able _____
9. count + less _____
10. spice + y _____
11. likely + hood _____
12. like + ed _____
13. stop + ing _____
14. contrive + ance _____
15. measure + able _____
16. omit + ing _____
17. profit + ing _____
18. hope + ful _____
19. premature + ly _____
20. notice + able _____
21. courage + ous _____
22. virtue + ous _____
23. use + able _____
24. commit + ing _____
25. commit + ment _____
26. fun + y _____
27. usual + ly _____
28. appease + ment _____
29. allot + ed _____
30. manage + able _____
31. commit + al _____
32. disclose + ure _____
33. nine + teen _____
34. emerge + ence _____

Test Yourself: Compound Words

A. Draw a line separating the parts of these compound words.

1. rainproof   4. quickstep   7. noseband   10. blackout 13. guideline

2. network   5. piecework 8. boardwalk   11. diehard   14. herdsman

3. manhandle 6. sleepwalk 9. hothead   12. freeway 15. homesick

B. Write the meanings of these words. Notice how the meaning of some of these compounds is different from the meanings of the two words that form them.

1. landmark _____

2. moneylender _____

3. moonlighting _____

4. mossback _____

5. backwash _____

6. mooncalf _____

7. pieplant _____

C. Combine each word in Column A with a word in Column B to form a compound word. The first one has been done for you.

Column A	Column B	Column A	Column B
1. pass	bird	6. hard	over
2. finger	fruit	7. port	powder
3. straight	word	8. gun	neck
4. grape	print	9. left	hole
5. humming	forward	10. leather	wood

Test Yourself: Plurals

A. Write the plurals for these words.

1. book _____   8. chorus _____

2. doctor _____   9. journey _____

3. dress _____   10. buzz _____

4. inch _____   11. community _____

5. valley _____   12. watch _____

6. monkey _____   13. proof _____

7. butterfly _____   14. crash _____

B. Some nouns have irregular plurals. See if you can write the plurals for these words. Check the dictionary if necessary.

1. child _____   8. woman _____

2. foot _____   9. alumnus _____

3. tooth _____   10. datum _____

4. mouse _____   11. memorandum _____

5. X _____   12. ABC _____

6. 10 _____   13. deer _____

7. man _____   14. louse _____

Test Yourself: Syllabication

A. Complete the following statements and give two examples of each.

1. When a single consonant comes between two vowels, the second syllable usually begins with the _____ . The first vowel has a long sound. Examples: _____

2. Sometimes when a single consonant comes between vowels, the second syllable will begin with the second vowel. Then the first vowel has a _____ sound. Examples: _____

3. When two like consonants come between two vowels, the first syllable usually ends after the _____ consonant. The first vowel has a short sound. The consonant in the _____ syllable is sounded and the consonant in the unaccented syllable is _____ . Examples: _____

4. When two unlike consonants come between two vowels, the first syllable usually ends with the _____ consonant. If a word has a prefix, suffix, or ending, the affix is a syllable by itself. The _____ word is generally accented. Examples: _____

_____

5. Words ending in *le* are usually divided so that the _____ _____ preceding the *le* will form the last syllable. Examples: _____

6. The letters *ck* are never separated when a word is divided into syllables. Usually the letters *ck* end the _____ .
Examples: _____

B. Write the number of syllables you hear in each word.

1. dictionary _____
2. biologist _____
3. conducive _____
4. diagram _____
5. magnolia _____
6. novelette _____

7. unpleasant _____
8. wonderful _____
9. reduce _____
10. pelican _____
11. hemisphere _____
12. frock _____

13. remembrance _____
14. suppression _____
15. noticeably _____
16. adventitious _____
17. morality _____
18. audience _____

C. Divide each of the following words into syllables by drawing a diagonal line between syllables.

1. seven
2. bottle
3. November
4. ego
5. magical
6. idea
7. butterscotch
8. aorta
9. appease
10. appetite

11. cyclometer
12. remnant
13. Ohio
14. create
15. visible
16. nullify
17. hospitality
18. abalone
19. arithmetic
20. aviation

21. communication
22. daughter
23. discontinuous
24. emotional
25. idiotic
26. neighborhood
27. originality
28. preinclination
29. abandonment
30. stupendous

D. Place the accent mark over the proper syllable.

1. man pow er
2. oc to pus
3. friend li ness
4. stu di o
5. au then tic

6. pu pil
7. un a ware
8. spec ta cle
9. stu pid i ty
10. trig o nom e try

11. vi bra tion
12. hos pi tal
13. for ceps
14. thim ble
15. No vem ber

E. Divide each of the following words into syllables. Mark accented syllables. For example: for bid´den.

1. kettle _____   6. thermostat _____

2. icicle _____   7. bicycle _____

3. lovable _____   8. ungracious _____

4. precocious _____   9. technical _____

5. society _____   10. duplicate _____

F. Many words of four or more syllables have a primary (´) and secondary (´) accent. Look in the dictionary and rewrite each word with a line between the syllables. Then mark the accented syllables. For example: ex´/is/ten´/tial.

1. continental _____   4. telephoto _____

2. independence _____   5. periscopic _____

3. obligation _____   6. readjustment _____

name _____ class _____ date _____

Test Yourself: Prefixes

A. Add a negative prefix to each word.

1. ___guarded 8. ___separable 15. ___religious 22. ___proper

2. ___ability 9. ___artistic 16. ___redeemable 23. ___adequate

3. ___learned 10. ___licit 17. ___legible 24. ___certain

4. ___reverent 11. ___efficient 18. ___moral 25. ___divided

5. ___regular 12. ___similar 19. ___named 26. ___literate

6. ___locked 13. ___material 20. ___mortal 27. ___opened

7. ___purity 14. ___sincere 21. ___reversible 28. ___divisible

B. Add the prefix re, pre, per, de, ex, mis, or dis to each root.

1. ___ply 8. ___note 15. ___jury 22. ___part

2. ___bar 9. ___courage 16. ___pert 23. ___amine

3. ___duct 10. ___tire 17. ___tense 24. ___sult

4. ___school 11. ___cursion 18. ___behave 25. ___secute

5. ___haust 12. ___fortune 19. ___touch 26. ___regard

6. ___treat 13. ___natal 20. ___own 27. ___vent

7. ___manent 14. ___fume 21. ___pendent 28. ___lead

C. Complete each sentence by writing the proper number on the line.

1. A quadrangle has _____ angles.

2. A bicycle has _____ wheels, whereas a tricycle has _____ , and a unicycle has only _____ .

3. When someone speaks in a monotone, he is speaking in _____ tone.

4. Carbon dioxide has _____ parts oxygen.

5. The Pentagon building has _____ sides.

6. A sextrain is a stanza that has _____ lines.

7. A centennial celebration celebrates a happening that is _____ years old.

8. A tripod has _____ legs.

9. On the Roman calendar November was the _____ month.

10. A septuagenarian is a person who is in his _____ year.

11. A university means several different colleges in _____ institution.

12. We are a monogamous society; by law each individual who is married can have only _____ spouse at a time.

13. When a magazine is published bimonthly, it appears every _____ months.

14. A decade is a period of _____ years.

15. In a quintet, the group consists of _____ persons.

Test Yourself: Suffixes

A. Add one of the following suffixes meaning *one who* to each of the
roots below: -ist, -ent, -ant, -ar, -or, -er, -ian.

1. act____	6. combat____	11. loyal____	16. beg____
2. teach____	7. edit____	12. stud____	17. conduct____
3. attend____	8. inspect____	13. correspond____	18. biolog____
4. serv____	9. li____	14. magic____	19. banjo____
5. music____	10. librar____	15. employ____	20. terror____

B. See how many new words you can make by adding suffixes to the
words listed below. For example: from *hand*, you could make *hand-
like, handed, handedness, handful, handily, handy, handiness, hand-
ier, handiest, handler, handling, handsome.*

1. fear _____

2. woman _____

3. brute _____

4. clown _____

5. nerve _____

6. tact _____

7. acid _____

8. sense _____

9. person _____

10. respect _____

Test Yourself: Roots

A. Below are five words formed from the same root. Study the word parts carefully and then fit the right word into each sentence.

democracy	*demo*, people + *cracy*, rule
demography	*demo*, people + *graphy*, write
demophile	*demo*, people + *phile*, love
demophobia	*demo*, people + *phobia*, fear
antidemocratic	*anti*, against + *demo*, people + *crat*, rule + *ic*, of

1. After living alone for many years, the old man developed _____

_____ .

2. In a _____ , all the people take an active part in government.

3. Because she did so much to help people, she was called a _____

_____ .

4. _____ is the study of the statistics about people.

5. A communist country is usually very _____.

B. Below are five words formed from the same root. Study the word parts carefully and then fit the right word into each sentence.

reversible	*re*, back + *vers*, turn + *ible*, capable of
introvert	*intro*, within + *vert*, turn
versatile	*vers*, turn + *ile*, like or pertaining to
controversial	*contro*, against + *vers*, turn + *ial*, like or pertaining to
version	*vers*, turn + *ion*, act of or quality of

1. The new _____of the story was different from the old one.

2. The _____ was more interested in himself than in others.

3. She was able to do many things, and was therefore _____
_____ .

4. The formula was not _____ ; the gas would be
deadly forever.

5. The subject was not discussed because it was so _____.

C. Below are five words formed from the same root. Study the word parts
    carefully and then fit the right word into each sentence.

recede	re, back + cede, go
concede	con, with + cede, go
procedure	pro, forward + cede, go + ure, act of
intercede	inter, between + cede, go
secede	se, apart + cede, go

1. After the rain stopped, the water in the river began to _____.

2. Lincoln was elected and the southern states began to _____.

3. The _____for assembling bicycles was in a small booklet.

4. The policeman had to _____to prevent the robbery.

5. Bob had to _____after hearing John's argument.

D. Complete each of the following sentences by using one of these
    words: *exported, extrovert, epidemic, convert, preceded, democrat,
    report, exceeding.*

1. A _____feels that a government should be ruled by the people.

2. The products were _____to many different countries.

3. Most of the natives suffered from the smallpox _____.

4. The students were asked to write a _____ on noise
pollution.

5. John was not shy or withdrawn; in fact, he was an _____.

6. As usual, "The Star-Spangled Banner" _____ the ball game.

7. The officer stopped him for _____ the speed limit.

8. Everyone tried to _____ Jack into becoming a club member.

Test Yourself: Word Parts

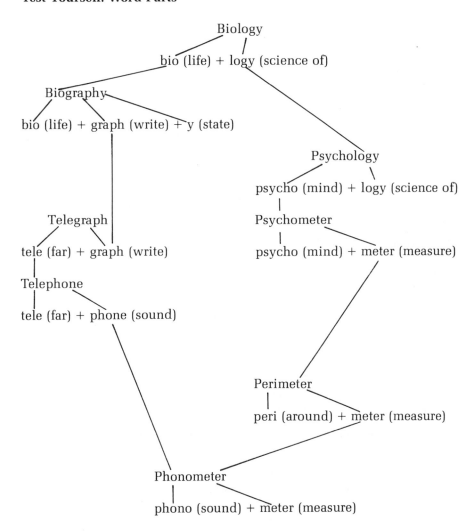

A. Write in the meaning of each word part or root.

1. phonology = phono _____ + logy _____

2. telemeter = tele _____ + meter _____

3. phonograph = phono _____ + graph _____

B. Listed below are several words formed from the Latin root *jacere*, meaning "to throw." Write the prefix, root, suffix, and the letter of the definition of each word in the proper column.

	Prefix	Root	Suffix	Definition
1. reject	_____	_____	_____	_____
2. injection	_____	_____	_____	_____
3. ejector	_____	_____	_____	_____
4. projection	_____	_____	_____	_____
5. interject	_____	_____	_____	_____
6. abjection	_____	_____	_____	_____
7. deject	_____	_____	_____	_____
8. conjecture	_____	_____	_____	_____
9. subject	_____	_____	_____	_____

Definitions

a. something that juts out

b. that which discharges or expels

c. state of being miserable; being at the lowest degree of feeling

d. to cast down in spirit

e. under authority or control of another

f. forcing a liquid into the body with a hypodermic needle

g. predicting from incomplete or uncertain evidence; guesswork

h. to interrupt; insert; interpose; to throw in between

i. to refuse to take; to throw back or discard

C. A word part such as *manu* is sometimes called a "combining form" because it is not a word by itself, but needs a prefix or suffix to form a complete word. In the exercises below, the meaning of the combining form is given. Use your dictionary and determine the meaning of the prefixes or suffixes of the words given as examples.

Combining Form	Prefix or Suffix	Meaning	Complete Word
graph (write)	epi	1. _____	epigraph
	para	2. _____	paragraph

	ic	3. _____ graphic
capt (take)	or	4. _____ captor
or	inter	5. _____ intercept
cept	ex	6. _____ except
plic (fold)	com	7. _____ complex
or	ation	8. _____ plication
plex	im (ate)	9. _____ implicate
mit (send)	ion	10. _____ mission
or	dis	11. _____ dismiss
miss	ad	12. _____ admit
tain (hold)	re	13. _____ retain
or	able	14. _____ tenable
ten	con	15. _____ contain
duct (lead)	in	16. _____ induct
	intro (ion)	17. _____ introduction
	ile	18. _____ ductile
pos (place, set)	trans	19. _____ transpose
or	post	20. _____ postpone
pon	tion	21. _____ position
tend (stretch)	in	22. _____ intend
or	ion	23. _____ tension
tens	dis	24. _____ distend
script (write)	post	25. _____ postscript
or	con	26. _____ conscript
scrib	in	27. _____ inscribe

Index of Skills

COMPREHENSION

STUDY SKILLS

VOCABULARY SKILLS

WORD ATTACK SKILLS

Answers to Selected Exercises

Page 4   Sound Sense: Vowels

1. short
2. long
3. nŏt
4. fŭn
5. wrȳ

6. ĭs
7. hē
8. ăt
9. stănd
10. cĭnch

11. brĭnk
12. whĕn
13. sprȳ
14. clŏg
15. shŏck

16. tĕmpt
17. stȳ
18. thătch
19. wrĕnch
20. stŭnt

Page 5   Check It

Topic sentence of first paragraph: Since criticism may be positive as well as negative, people who criticize us often think they are helping us. Second paragraph: There are many ways of reacting to personal criticism by others.

Page 6   Sound Sense: Vowels

1. two
2. one
3. long, silent
4. plănt

5. rēlȳ
6. lŭnch
7. lămb
8. sōlō

9. rōdĕnt
10. drȳ

Pages 7–8   Check It

The sentence that best expresses the main idea is 3.

Page 8   Sound Sense: Vowels

These words should have been circled: race, fine, tone, made, tube, these, game, time, those

Pages 10–11   Words You Need

1. a   2. c   3. b   4. c   5. a   6. c   7. b   8. b   9. a   10. c   11. a   12. b

Pages 16–17   Check It

1. b   2. a   3. b   4. c   5. c   6. a   7. c   8. b   9. c   10. b   11. c   12. b

Page 18   Can You Read a Bus Schedule?

1. 15 hours 5 minutes   2. 12:45 P.M.

UNIT TWO

Page 31   Sound Sense: Digraphs

1. th   2. ch   3. ch   4. sh   5. th   6. sh   7. wh, ch   8. ph   9. ph
10. gh

Page 31   Sound Sense: Silent Consonants

1. b   2. p   3. k   4. w   5. n   6. g   7. l   8. t   9. l

Page 31   Sound Sense: Consonant Blends

1. fl	5. cl	9. cl	13. str	17. scr
2. dr,pl	6. dr,ft	10. gr,nd,st,nd	14. spl	18. str
3. gl,nd	7. fr,nd	11. br	15. str	19. spl
4. sp,nk	8. cr,sp	12. sl,nt	16. scr	20. spr

Page 35   True or False

1. T   2. F   3. F   4. T   5. T

Page 37   Words You Need

1. c   2. c   3. b   4. c   5. b   6. a   7. b   8. c   9. a   10. c

Pages 41, 42 and 43   Check It

1. c   2. a   3. c   4. a   5. a   6. a   7. b   8. b   9. c   10. c

Page 48   Words You Need

1. c   2. a   3. c   4. a   5. c   6. a   7. b   8. c

Page 53 True or False

1. T   2. T   3. T   4. F   5. F   6. T   7. F   8. T

UNIT THREE

Pages 57–58   True or False

1. F   2. F   3. F   4. T   5. F

Pages 59–60   Check It

1. c   2. b

Page 62   Words You Need

1. b   2. c   3. a   4. c   5. a   6. a   7. c   8. c

Pages 67–68   Check It

1. c   2. a   3. c   4. b   5. c   6. a   7. c   8. b

Pages 72–73   Finding Words in the Dictionary

fourth letters: 4, 1, 3, 2

Page 73   Using Guide Words

enhance–enroll 1. B   2. X   3. X   4. A   5. X

Page 75   Parts Department: Roots

auto, self + bio, life + graphy, writing

1. psycho, logy, science of the mind
2. phil, anthrop, y, love of man

261

3. mono, gam, ist, one who is married to only one person at a time
4. phono, graph, writing in sound

UNIT FOUR

Pages 79-80   True or False

1. F   2. F   3. T   4. F   5. T

Page 80   Sound Sense: Diphthongs

The following words should be circled: 1, 4, 13, 14, 15
The following words should be underlined: 3, 5, 8, 9, 11, 12

Pages 81–82   True or False

1. T   2. T   3. F   4. F   5. F

Page 82   Parts Department: Suffixes

1. consonant   2. vowel   3. tamed   4. changing   5. traceable

Pages 83–84   True or False

1. F   2. T   3. T   4. F   5. F

Page 84   Parts Department: Suffixes

1. The following words complete the statement: consonant, vowel, consonant. The correct forms of the words are: 2. committed   3. preferring
4. prohibiting   5. opener

Page 85   Pronunciation and the Dictionary

1. Great spenders are bad losers. —Franklin
2. Life is made up of sobs, sniffles, and smiles, with sniffles predominating. —O. Henry

Page 94   Would You Believe?

emigrant: one who moves out
immigrant: one who moves in
migratory: a worker who moves from place to place

Page 95   Reading the Newspaper

1. C8   2. C11–14   3. A8   4. C1–6   5. B4

UNIT FIVE

Page 99   True or False

1. F   2. F   3. T   4. T   5. T

Page 100   True or False

1. F   2. T   3. F   4. F

Page 101   True or False

1. F   2. F   3. T   4. F   5. T

Page 104   Reading a Table of Contents

1. 1   2. 2   3. 9   4. 33   5. 37

Page 107   Sound Sense: The Sounds of S

1. suit   2. sure   3. lose   4. treasure

Page 107   Sound Sense: The Sounds of C

1. S   2. S   3. H   4. H   5. S

Page 108   Words You Need

1. b   2. a   3. a   4. c   5. a   6. b   7. b   8. c   9. a

Page 112   True or False

1. T   2. F   3. F   4. F   5. F   6. T   7. F

UNIT SIX

Page 121   Sound Sense: The ô Sound

1. aw   3. aw   5. aw   6. al   7. au   8. al   9. au   10. al

Page 122   Sound Sense: The Sounds of G

1. H   2. S   3. H   4. S

Page 122   Sound Sense: The Sounds of W

1. C   2. C   3. V   4. V   5. C

Page 123   True or False

1. F   2. T   3. T   4. T   5. T

Page 124   Sound Sense: The Sounds of Y

hy̆mn, lȳre, youth, cȳcle

Page 125   Check It

1. c   2. b

Page 127   Figures of Speech

1. M   2. S   3. S   4. M   5. M   6. M   7. S   8. S   9. M

Page 128   Words You Need

1. b   2. b   3. b   4. b   5. c   6. b   7. a   8. b   9. c   10. c

Page 133 Check It

1. a 2. a 3. c 4. b 5. a 6. c 7. b 8. c

Page 134 Words You Need

1. a 2. d 3. c 4. c 5. d 6. c 7. d 8. c 9. b 10. b

Page 139 Check It

1. c 2. b 3. b 4. c 5. b 6. b 7. c 8. c 9. b

UNIT SEVEN

Pages 145–146 True or False

1. F 2. F 3. F 4. T 5. T

Page 146 Sound Sense: The Schwa Sound

pilot ago student razor pleasant
oblige mystery lesson human comma

Page 148 Check it: Topic Sentences

(1) The Point Reyes National Seashore is truly a paradise for nature enthusiasts.
(2) In many cases the practice of transplanting fish from one geographic area to another works to the benefit of good sport fishing. And: In some cases, then, the practice of transplanting fish has hindered the enjoyment of sport fishermen.

Page 148 Sound Sense: Homonyms

1. fare 2. flea 3. choir 4. pane

Page 149   True or False

1. F 2. T 3. F 4. F 5. T

Pages 150–151 Figures of Speech: Personification and Hyperbole

1. P 2. H 3. P 4. P 5. H 6. H 7. P 8. P 9. P 10. H

Page 151 Words You Need

1. a 2. b 3. b 4. a 5. c

Page 158 Check It

1. b 2. b 3. c 4. b 5. c 6. c 7. c 8. b

Page 162 Would You Believe?

1. f 2. d 3. e 4. h 5. k 6. b 7. o 8. n 9. l 10. g 11. c 12. i
13. j 14. m 15. a

UNIT EIGHT

Page 165   True or False

1. T   2. T   3. F

Page 166   Parts Department: The Syllable

1. 1, 1, 3, 5, 1, 2
2. vowel
3. she∉ting, 2
4. appro∕ch, 2

5. moment, 2
6. caterpillar, 4
7. microscop∉, 3
8. yesterda∦, 3

Page 167   True or False

1. F   2. T   3. F   4. F   5. T

Page 169   Parts Department: Combined Forms

The meanings are: moving, writing, rule.

Page 170   Parts Department: The Vowel Syllable

1. a̲bout, 2   2. 3   3. el_e_phant, 3

Page 171   True or False

1. T   2. T   3. F   4. F   5. T

Page 173   Irony, Oxymorons, and Puns

1. O   2. I   3. I   4. O   5. P   6. I   7. P   8. P, I   9. I   10. P

Page 173   Would You Believe?

1. skillful, knowing   2. rustic, happy, innocent   3. tricky, crafty

Page 174   Words You Need

1. b   2. a   3. c   4. c   5. b   6. b   7. b   8. c   9. a   10. c

Pages 177–178   Check It

1. a   2. c   3. c   4. b   5. a   6. c   7. b   8. c   9. c   10.a

Page 180   Words You Need

1. b   2. a   3. c   4. b   5. c   6. a   7. b   8. c   9. b   10. a

Pages 185–186   Check It

1. b   2. c   3. b   4. a   5. c   6. b   7. b   8. c

Pages 187   Would You Believe?

a. feather in my cap, 2
b. in the groove, 6
c. hook, line and sinker, 9
d. hold a candle, 1
e. killed the fatted calf, 4

f. odds and ends, 3
g. fish or cut bait, 7
h. dark horse, 10
i. scuttlebutt, 5
j. taken down a peg or two, 8

UNIT NINE

Page 191   True or False

1. F   2. T   3. F   4. T

Page 193   True or False

1. T   2. F   3. F   4. F

Pages 195–196   True or False

1. F   2. T   3. F   4. F   5. T

Page 196   Parts Department: Dividing Words into Syllables

The following words complete the statement: consonant, consonant
The rewritten words are: sam·ple, trem′·ble, nee′·dle, tur′·tle, am′·ple, peo′·ple.

Pages 196–197 Parts Department: Adding Prefixes and Suffixes to Roots

6, in, spire   3, con, spirat, or   2, tran(s), spire

Page 198   Words You Need

1. a   2. c   3. b   4. a   5. c   6. b   7. b   8. b   9. c

Pages 205–206   Check It

1. c   2. c   3. c   4. a   5. b   6. c

Page 207   Alliteration and Onomatopoeia

1. onomatopoeia   2. alliteration   3. both   4. onomatopoeia

Page 208   Words You Need

1. b   2. a   3. c   4. c   5. b   6. c

Page 212   True or False

1. F   2. F   3. F   4. T   5. T   6. F   7. F   8. T   9. F   10. F